Franz Kafka

Michigan Studies in Comparative Jewish Cultures emphasizes the dynamic interplay of Jews as historical subjects, Judaism as faith and practice, and Jewishness as a repertoire of cultural practices with other peoples and cultures. It addresses a wide range of cultural forms, including art and theater, music and film, in relation to literature and history.

Series Editors:
Jonathan Freedman, University of Michigan
Anita Norich, University of Michigan
Scott Spector, University of Michigan

Nothing Happened: Charlotte Salomon and an Archive of Suicide
Darcy C. Buerkle

Languages of Modern Jewish Cultures: Comparative Perspectives
Joshua L. Miller and Anita Norich, editors

Never Better! The Modern Jewish Picaresque
Miriam Udel

Franz Kafka: Subversive Dreamer
Michael Löwy, translated by Inez Hedges

Strangers in Berlin: Modern Jewish Literature between East and West, 1919–1933
Rachel Seelig

Franz Kafka

SUBVERSIVE DREAMER

Michael Löwy

Translated by Inez Hedges

UNIVERSITY OF MICHIGAN PRESS
ANN ARBOR

Published in the United States of America by the
University of Michigan Press
Manufactured in the United States of America
⊗ Printed on acid-free paper

2019   2018   2017   2016   4   3   2   1

A CIP catalog record for this book is available from the British Library.

Library of Congress Cataloging-in-Publication Data

Names: Löwy, Michael, 1938– author. | Hedges, Inez, 1947– translator.

Title: Franz Kafka : subversive dreamer / Michael Lowy ; translated by InezHedges.
Other titles: Franz Kafka, rãeveur insoumis. English
Description: Ann Arbor : University of Michigan Press, [2016] | Series:
Michigan studies in comparative Jewish cultures | Includes index.
Identifiers: LCCN 2016019931| ISBN 9780472053094 (paperback : acid-free paper) |
    ISBN 9780472073092 (hardcover : acid-free paper) | ISBN 9780472121793 (e-book)
Subjects: LCSH: Kafka, Franz, 1883–1924—Criticism and interpretation.
Classification: LCC PT2621.A26 Z7691813 2016 | DDC 833/.912—dc23
LC record available at https://lccn.loc.gov/2016019931

CONTENTS

TRANSLATOR'S INTRODUCTION

Every decade since the 1920s has experienced its own version of the "Kafkaesque." In the twenty-first century, Löwy's readings update and contemporize what Kafka brings to our new experiences of despotism, cruelty, and injustice, while insisting that the author urges not resignation in defeat but resistance.

What emerges from Löwy's remarkable essay is the image of Kafka as a mind and spirit whose lucid vision allowed him to pierce with hallucinatory accuracy the intransigent paradoxes of human life. He is the eternally "disinherited son," as he says in his "Letter to My Father." But this is only half of it. He also, rebelliously, disinherits himself by refusing the authority of the patriarch—the state as well as the father.

Kafka and his protagonists—Karl Rossmann (*The Man Who Disappeared*), Joseph K. (*The Trial*), K. (*The Castle*), and many others—have allies. Sometimes they are strong women (Löwy finds echoes here of Kafka's own sister Ottla). Always when the character fails, Löwy argues, this is presented as a negative example not to be followed. Kafka shows that we must never acquiesce to authority. In support of his claim, Löwy takes the reader on a meticulous reexamination of the novels and stories, the diaries, notebooks, and unpublished writings, as well as the reports of Kafka's biographers.

Löwy's writing style is a pleasure to read in the original French. I hope I have done it justice, at least in part. One of the challenges was to decide which English translations of Kafka to use. Just as every era rediscovers its own version of the "Kafkaesque," some of the older translations into English no longer fit our current usage. In most cases I have been able to find newer versions that convey more readily the energy of the German original. I have also tracked down and used English versions of much of the secondary literature from which Löwy quotes.

For Michael Löwy the great drama of Kafka's life and work is the struggle against patriarchy in all its forms—a struggle in which his weapons are his writing and his anarchist sympathies, but one for which he also marshals the deepest impulses of his unconscious life. Michael Löwy sees Kafka as a dreamer, but a subversive one.

One final note: The French word *libertaire* refers to partisans of anarchist, semianarchist. or antiauthoritarian forms of *socialism*. *Libertarian*, when it appears in the translation, has obviously nothing to do with the US group of self-styled "libertarians," whom Löwy correctly characterizes as "right-wing partisans of extreme free-market *capitalism*, and therefore opposed to any form of state intervention, in particular welfare-state initiatives."

INTRODUCTION
Chains of Official Paper

Can one say anything new about Kafka? This book tries to take up the challenge. The time has come to consider his works from a different vantage point, in order to examine their fascinating power of insubordination.

In his famous essay on Kafka, Walter Benjamin warned (in many cases to no avail) that Kafka "took all conceivable precautions against the interpretation of his writings. One has to find one's way in them circumspectly, cautiously, and warily."[1] The chapters that follow should be seen as a cautious and tentative essay, a hypothesis in need of corroboration, and a possible point of departure for further study.

Commentaries on Kafka constitute an ever-growing mass of documents that, with time, have taken on the appearance of a Tower of Babel—an infinite enterprise in a confusion of languages. Is it by accident that women have often provided the most interesting readings of Kafka? I mention with the greatest admiration authors like Hannah Arendt, Marthe Robert, Rosemarie Ferenczi, and Marina Cavarocci-Arbib, whose works rise above the gray and indistinct mass of most of the "secondary literature." I don't always agree with their analysis, but I have mostly relied on their contributions, while developing my own thoughts in yet another direction.

One can classify the studies of the Prague author according to six major approaches:

1. Strictly literary readings that limit themselves deliberately to the text and ignore the "context"
2. Biographical, psychological, and psychoanalytic readings
3. Theological, metaphysical, and religious readings
4. Readings from the point of view of Kafka's Jewish identity
5. Sociopolitical readings
6. Postmodern readings, which usually arrive at the conclusion that the meaning of Kafka's writings is "undecidable"

These interpretations are of unequal value: some of them contain important insights, but many tend to reduce the literary work to a preestablished model, interpreting situations and characters as purveyors of a symbolic or allegorical message. The multifarious secondary literature has been expanded in recent years by the growing body of tertiary studies: the analysis of the different interpretations of the Prague author. Perhaps there will someday be yet another level—a quaternary literature!

In another well-known passage from his essay, Walter Benjamin remarks that there are two ways to miss Kafka completely: the natural and the supernatural—in other words, the psychoanalytical and the religious approaches. This remark seems profoundly accurate to me. Although these two dimensions are not absent in his works, they are *aufgehoben*, in the dialectical sense of the term: negated-preserved-transcended. For example, though the oedipal conflict—the violent conflict with the father—is clearly present in the works of Kafka, all his art consists precisely in going beyond this psychological aspect into an imaginary universe in which the questioning of authority is generalized. The same is true for Judaism: the Jewish condition is an essential point of departure, which is nonetheless "negated-preserved" into a universal problematic. As Marthe Robert observes, the condition of the Prague Jews, enclosed in a "ghetto of invisible walls," becomes, in the works of Kafka—especially in his three posthumous novels—"the outline of an infinitely more general condition."[2] As for the theological element, I will try to show that, though present, it is "negative."

Finally we have to consider the purely literary reading. It's certainly true that Kafka lived only for literature: it was his obsession, his raison d'être, his only salvation. It was his way of responding to a fallen world. Taking this as their point of departure—from their reading of the *Diaries* and the letters—many critics have fallen into the trap of making literature the object, the content, the warp and woof of his writings, as though they were an elaborate allegory of the writing itself, in an infinite refraction of mirrors. But this perception is illusory. Robert Musil also was obsessed with his own oeuvre, yet literature is not its object, and his imaginary Cacania is not an allegory for his own writings. The point of Kafka's oeuvre is not writing as such, but the relation between the individual and the world. Naturally, one or the other novella can have as its subject the literary work itself: this is probably the case with "Odradek" in the famous parable "The Cares of a Family Man"—as shown by the brilliant analysis of Marthe Robert in *As Lonely as Franz Kafka*. But it would be vain to apply this model to his novels and to the whole of his writings.

Considering the enormous volume of secondary literature on Kafka, why add yet another stone to this hermeneutic pyramid? My contribution falls within the "sociopolitical" sphere, but it attempts to flesh out other levels, thanks to a "red thread" that establishes connections between the revolt against the father, the religion of liberty (of heterodox Jewish inspiration), and protest inspired by anarchism against the murderous power of the bureaucratic apparatus: the thread of *antiauthoritarianism*. In his 1929 article on surrealism, Benjamin wrote: "Since Bakunin, Europe has lacked a radical concept of freedom. The Surrealists have one."[3] This pronouncement applies perfectly to Franz Kafka.

I will attempt to follow this red thread in chronological order, starting from certain biographical facts that are often neglected, such as the relations between Kafka and the Prague anarchist circles; I will then analyze the three great, unfinished novels and some of the most important novellas. I will also consider the fragmentary writings, the parables, the letters, and the diaries in an attempt to shed light on the major literary texts, but without considering Kafka's oeuvre in its totality. I have not tried to interpret his earliest writings—those before 1912—nor the last, such as "Josephine the Singer," "Investigations of a Dog," and so on. I cannot say whether these texts, or certain of the parables, aphorisms, and fragments are consistent with my hypothesis.

I don't think I am claiming too much in saying that this reading of Kafka—based on following the "Ariadne thread" of the desire for liberty through the Kafka labyrinth—is a new one. In any case, I have found nothing like it in the secondary literature. What I found in some interpretations are suggestions, fragments, intuitions, and some passages that I quote—sometimes out of their original context—in order to develop my argument. Nowhere did I find a systematic analysis of Kafka's oeuvre from the point of view of the passion for antiauthoritarianism that runs through it like an electric current. Thanks to this way of reading, the pieces of the puzzle seem to fall into place and the principal writings of Kafka appear to exhibit a very great *coherence*. Of course, this is not a coherence of doctrine, but of sensibility.

This interpretation has no claim to being exhaustive. It is rather an attempt to *highlight the incredibly critical and subversive dimension of Kafka's oeuvre*, which has so often been unacknowledged. It is not at all a reading based on consensus, and it will not fail to create controversy since it differs so radically from the usual reading of Kafka by literary critics. My effort is largely influenced by Walter Benjamin, not only by his 1934 essay on Kafka but also by his 1940 theses "On the Concept of History." In the sixth thesis, he warns the historian as follows: "Every age must strive anew to wrest tradition away from the conformism that is working to overpower it."[4] This book is intended as a small contribution toward that goal.

The "political" reading I propose here is of course only partial: the universe of Kafka is too rich, complex, and multiform to be reduced to a simple formula. Despite the pertinence of any interpretation, his oeuvre retains all of its disquieting mystery and its singular oneiric character, a sort of "waking dream state" inspired by the logic of the marvelous. To paraphrase André Breton, poetry always retains "an indestructible kernel of night."

The word "political" is in any case inappropriate. What interests Kafka is a thousand leagues from what is normally designated by that word: political parties, elections, institutions, constitutional regimes, and so on. "Critical" might be a better term. This critical dimension is often eclipsed by a kind of academic interpretation. At the same time, it is probably what millions of modern readers associate with Kafka, who has become the synonym of anxiety in the face of the system of bureaucracy.

To characterize the oppressive power of this system, Kafka provides a striking image: "The chains of tormented mankind are made out of official papers."[5] The German term *Kanzleipapier* is hard to translate: some translators use the term "red tape," but this does not give a sense of the richness of the term's origin. *Kanzlei* is usually translated as "office"; it has its source in medieval Latin, *cancelleria*, which describes a place surrounded by bars—*cancelli*—where official documents are prepared. It's a word that one finds often in Kafka's novels *The Trial* and *The Castle*, to describe the places ruled by the officials—places that are always surrounded by high *cancelli*, whether visible or invisible, and which keep out common mortals. These *Kanzleipapiere* are written or printed documents: official forms, records of accusation, or decisions of the Tribunal. *Writing* is therefore the medium though which the governing officials exercise their power. Kafka's answer is to use the same medium, but to reverse the procedure: his writing is one of literary or poetic freedom that subverts the pretensions of the powerful.

The image of "paper chains" seems also to have a double meaning: it suggests at once the oppressive character of the bureaucratic system that enslaves individuals through official documents, and the precarious nature of the chains, which could easily be torn apart, if people wanted to free themselves.

Kafka has often been accused—by Georg Lukács, Günther Anders, and others—of being a radical pessimist and of preaching fatalism and resignation. However, in a letter to Oscar Pollak of January 27, 1904, he explains his conception of the role of literature: "Why would we read a book unless it awakens us like a blow to the head . . . every book should be like an axe that opens up our frozen sea."[6] This doesn't sound much like a call for resignation.

Postscript

The paternal branch of my family, the Löwys, came from Bohemia like the maternal branch of Kafka's family (his mother was Julia Löwy). The name was a common one in the Austro-Hungarian Empire, and as far as I know there is no link between the two families, except for the (mythic) one of belonging to the vast tribe of the Levites, scribes and inscribers of parchments about the Eternal . . .

I first heard of Kafka during my high school years in Brazil at a lecture by Maurício Tragtenberg on "the bureaucracy in Kafka's *The Castle.*" Maurício was a young Jewish Brazilian intellectual, a self-educated libertarian Marxist (he would later have a university career). I don't remember the particulars of his lecture, but he advanced the notion that Kafka's novel was one of the most important critical analyses of the meaning of the powers of bureaucracy in modern society; my book owes much to this long-ago but unforgettable talk by my late friend.

Of all the members of Kafka's Prague circle, the only one I had the opportunity to meet was Samuel Hugo Bergmann, his classmate and the first witness of his socialist leanings. I was among a group of Hebrew students that he hosted at his house in Jerusalem one Saturday afternoon in 1963. He shared with us some reflections on modern life, based on an everyday scene that he had witnessed: two lovers in a park completely absorbed by the words . . . of a transistor radio they were listening to. Bergman commented that our society was beginning to lose its capacity for dialogue and mutual listening—that we were experiencing a crisis in human communication, a decline in direct human interaction that was being replaced by impersonal devices. It was an unforgettable lesson in the cultural criticism (*Kulturkritik*) of modern life, in the best tradition of the German-Jewish romanticism of Central Europe.

The origin of my research on Kafka goes back to an essay from the 1960s, which has a curious history. It was published with the title "Kafka and Anarchism" in Hebrew in the April 1967 issue of the Tel Aviv review *Beayot Beinleumiot* (*International Problems*). A few months later, it was translated into Yiddish for the *New York Freie Arbeiter Stimme* (*Free Workers' Voice*), an American socialist libertarian newspaper. Then came a Spanish translation in the Argentine periodical *Tierra y Libertad* (*Land and Liberty*) and another English one in 1972 in the form of a booklet and attributed to a certain "Mijal Levy" (an Argentinian transliteration of the Yiddish?). I knew nothing about these translations. But, in 1981, I published a revised and corrected edition in French, with the same title, in a collection of essays honoring Lucien Goldmann.[7] This first essay owes much to the biography of the young Kafka by Klaus Wagenbach, though it already represents an attempt at an interpretation of Kafka's oeuvre.

I came back to Kafka in 1988, in my book *Redemption and Utopia* (translated into English in 1992), which takes up and expands the themes of this first attempt. I had the chance to discuss this version with the late Gershom Scholem, who was interested in my thesis without necessarily agreeing with it. I continued to work on Kafka during the 1990s. Shorter versions of some of those chapters have appeared in the reviews *Archives de sciences sociales des religions* (CNRS, Paris), *L'Homme et la société* (Paris), *Diogène* (UNESCO, Paris), *Réfractions* (Lyon), *Analogon* (Prague), and *Salmandra* (Madrid).

If I have decided to take up this subject once again, it is out of a conviction that Kafka is relevant as never before, and more readable than ever in the anguished beginning of our twenty-first century—he carries with him what Walter Benjamin called the *Jetztzeit*—"the present time." Today, even more than in the time of Kafka, this subversive dreamer, "the chains of tortured mankind are made out of official papers."

CHAPTER 1

"DON'T FORGET KROPOTKIN!"
Kafka and Antiauthoritarian Socialism

It should be clearly stated that one cannot reduce Kafka's oeuvre to any particular political doctrine. Kafka doesn't make *speeches*; he creates characters and situations, attitudes, an *atmosphere*. The symbolic world of literature cannot be reduced to the discursive world of ideologies; the literary work is not an *abstract conceptual system* in the service of philosophical or political doctrines, but the creation of a *concrete imaginary universe* of people and things.[1]

However, this does not prevent us from investigating the passages, the footbridges, the subterranean connections between his principal writings and his antiauthoritarian spirit, his libertarian sensibility,[2] and his socialist sympathies. These are the avenues that provide access to what we might call his *inner landscape*.

Kafka's socialist inclinations manifested themselves at an early date: according to his childhood friend Hugo Bergmann, Kafka wore a red carnation in his buttonhole in order to advertise his political leanings. Their friendship suffered during their last year at school (1900–1901) because, as Bergmann writes, "his socialism and my Zionism were too strong."[3] These disagreements didn't prevent them from reacting in the same way to German nationalism. When, during a meeting of the Prague German students' union (of which both of them were members), they remained seated during the singing of the traditional "Wacht am Rhein" (a nationalist song), they were immediately thrown out.[4]

Was kind of socialism was this? There are no reports of connections between the young Kafka and Czech or Austrian social democracy. The same is true for the Communist Party of the new Czech Republic in the postwar years—even if one of the founders of the party, Stanislas K. Neumann, knew him and published "The Stoker" in a Czech literary review in 1920. In any case, the socialist engagement of Kafka mentioned by Bergmann dates from before October 1917.

Kafka expressed interest in the Russian Revolution. In a letter to Milena of August 29 and 30, 1920, he includes an article on Bolshevism that made a strong impression, as he says, "on my body, my nerves, my blood." According to the editors of the new edition of the letters to Milena, he is talking about an article by Bertrand Russell titled "On Bolshevist Russia" that appeared in the *Prager Tagblatt* on August 25, 1920. But Kafka adds something here that seems important to me: "In truth, I haven't adopted it wholesale, I've first transcribed it for my own orchestra."[5] This is a remark that applies generally to any "influence" that Kafka felt: he is never the passive recipient; rather, he engages in a selective reelaboration, a personal "putting to music."[6] Let's take a closer look at this article by Bertrand Russell, in order to better understand Kafka's own position. The text is the first of a series of five published by *The Nation* in July and August 1920, a series that purports to offer a fair assessment of the Soviet government. The series emphasizes, on the one hand, the sincerity of the Bolsheviks, whom Russell compares to the Cromwell Puritans because of their "combination of democracy and religious faith" as well as their "stern political-moral purpose"; and on the other, their tendency toward dictatorship and intolerance. In his letter to Milena, Kafka explains that he has torn off the end of the article, because "it contains accusations against the Communists." Which ones? In the article's final paragraph, Russell criticizes what he calls the Bolsheviks' imperialist tendencies (their reconquest of Asiatic Russia), and he predicts that "they will increasingly resemble any other Asiatic government." Kafka objected to these accusations, which, he says, "don't belong in this context."[7]

His point of view becomes clearer in another letter to Milena dated September 7: "I don't know whether you properly understood my remark about the article on Bolshevism. What the author takes exception to is for me the highest possible praise on earth (*höchste auf Erden mögliche Lob*)."[8] What criticism of Russell's is he referring to? Not to the one expressed in the paragraph he tore out, since Milena wouldn't have seen it; he is addressing, rather, a more general argument in the article. The philosopher had many criticisms of the Russian Communists, but what seemed to him most dangerous was their project to extend the revolution on a global scale. "The true communist is thoroughly international. Lenin, for example . . . is not more concerned with the interests of Russia than with those of other countries; Russia is, at the moment, the protagonist of the social revolution, and as such valuable to the world, but Lenin would sacrifice Russia rather than the revolution if the alternative should ever arise."[9] In other words, what Kafka finds to praise in the Russian revolutionaries is exactly what Russell reproaches them for—their radical internationalist engagement. We will see that this "cosmopolitan socialist" sensibility of Kafka's is confirmed by other testimonials.[10]

Gustav Janouch quotes him as follows, from a conversation in 1920: "In Russia men are trying to construct an absolutely just world. It is a religious matter." Kafka sees Bolshevism as a kind of religion, and the blockades and other forms of intervention against Russia seem to him to presage "the great and cruel religious wars, which will sweep across the world."[11] These comments are evidence of an interest—laced with criticism—in the Soviet experience; but there is no proof of any relationship between the author and the Communist movement. There are no reports of his ever having attended a meeting of Czech Communists, and in his personal writings—letters and diaries—he never discusses authors who represent this particular political view.[12]

On the other hand, many reports by his contemporaries mention the sympathy that he had for the *Czech libertarian socialists* as well as his participation in some of their activities. It's therefore here that we should concentrate our investigations if we want to understand the adherence (described by Bergmann as "too strong") of the young Kafka to socialism. In the early 1930s, during his research for his novel *Stefan Rott* (1931), Max Brod obtained some information from one of the founders of the Czech anarchist movement, Michael Kacha. According to Kacha, Kafka attended the meetings of the socialist, libertarian, antimilitarist, and anticlerical Klub Mladych (Young People's Club)—a club that was attended by several Czech writers such as Stanislas K. Neumann, Michal Mares, Jaroslav Hasek, and Frana Sramek. Max Brod included this information (which he claimed was "confirmed by other sources" without, unfortunately, giving details) in his novel, where he wrote that Kafka took part in the meetings: "He didn't utter a word, the whole evening . . . Kacha liked him, and called him a 'klidas,' that is, a 'close-mouth'" (in Prague-Czech slang). Max Brod never questioned the truthfulness of this report, which he cites again in his biography of Kafka.[13]

The second report comes from the anarchist writer Michal Mares, who had met Kafka in the street. There are two slightly different versions of his text: the first appeared in 1946 in a Czech periodical and scarcely got any attention; the second, more detailed and probably more accurate, was published as an appendix to Klaus Wagenbach's 1958 book on Kafka's youth. This was the first work to highlight the connections between the author and the centers of Prague socialist libertarianism. Mares states that at his invitation Kafka came to a protest against the execution in October 1909 of Francisco Ferrer, the Spanish anarchist educator. Then in 1910–1912, he took part in anarchist meetings on free love, on the Paris Commune, on peace, and in a protest against the execution of the militant Parisian Liabeuf organized by the Young People's Club, the anticlerical and antimilitarist

Vilem Körber Association, and the Czech anarchist movement. In the course of these meetings, he is said to have met his former schoolmate Rudolf Illowy, as well as writers and poets like Stanislas K. Neumann, Frana Sramek, Karel Toman, and Jaroslav Hasek. He is even reported to have paid bail to liberate his friend from prison after both were arrested during the protest against the execution of Liabeuf. Like Kacha, Mares mentions Kafka's silence: "As far as I know, Kafka didn't belong to any of the anarchist clubs; yet one can say that he felt a deep sympathy with them, as a person with a profound social consciousness. He was very interested in such meetings (which he often attended) but never took part in the debates himself." Mares also reports that Kafka read Kropotkin's *Words of a Rebel* (which he had given him).[14]

Another unpublished version of Mares's recollections contains the following remark: "I remember the anger Kafka expressed toward young Americans upon learning that the generous and courageous Emma Goldman had been undressed and tarred and feathered in public."[15] Apparently, Mares has combined two different events: the first, from 1909, was the booing of Emma Goldman during a lecture that she gave at the University of Michigan (though she still managed to finish); the second, from 1911, was the kidnapping of her friend Ben Breitman by a band of San Diego vigilantes who did manage to tar and feather him. Kafka's interest in Emma Goldman at this time is due not only to his research on the United States for his first novel, but also to his sympathy for, and attraction to, courageous and rebellious women who fearlessly confront obstacles. There are many references to these rebellious female figures, whose archetype is no doubt to be found in his sister Ottla's resistance to the authority of the father—as he states in his letters and writings.

The third document we have is Gustav Janouch's *Conversations with Kafka*, which appeared first in 1951 and then in a considerably expanded edition in 1968. In this account of conversations held during Kafka's last years (after 1920), we can read that Kafka retained his sympathy for the anarchists. Not only does he call the Czech anarchists "so nice and friendly, that one has to believe every word they say"[16]—the political and social ideas that he expresses during these conversations have a decidedly libertarian socialist bent. For instance, his view of capitalism as a hierarchical system of domination is close to anarchism's insistence on the authoritarian character of that system.[17] He makes this explicit during a debate with Janouch about a caricature by George Grosz, representing Capital as a fat man sitting on the money of the poor. According to Kafka, the image is "both true and false. It is true only in one sense. . . . The fat man oppresses the poor man within the conditions of a given system. But he is not the system itself. He is not even its master. On the contrary, the fat man also is in chains, which the picture does not show. . . . Capitalism is a system of relationships, which go from inside to out, from outside to in, from above to below, and from below to above. Everything is relative, everything is in chains. Capitalism is a condition both of the world and of the soul."[18]

In the same way, his skepticism with regard to the organized labor movement seems inspired by the anarchist suspicion of political parties and institutions. Behind the workers who parade in street demonstrations he detects "the secretaries, officials, professional politicians, all the modern satraps for whom they are preparing the way to power. . . . The Revolution evaporates and leaves behind only the slime of a new bureaucracy. The chains of tormented mankind are made out of official papers."[19] What revolution was he thinking of when he said this? That of October 1917 or those of Germany and Austria in 1918–1919? It's impossible to say. In any case, the sentence about chains of official paper applies not only to the tragic destiny of revolutions, but also to the phenomenon of bureaucracy in all of its manifestations.

The second edition of *Conversations with Kafka* is based on the complete version of his notes that Janouch lost after the war but later recovered. Here Janouch quotes the following exchange with Kafka:

"You studied Ravachol's life?"

"Yes, and not only Ravachol's but the lives of various other anarchists. I went deeply into the lives and ideas of Godwin, Proudhon, Stirner, Bakunin, Kropotkin, Tucker and Tolstoy, frequented various circles and meetings, and devoted much time and money to the subject. In 1910 I took part in the meetings of the anarchist 'Club of the Young' which, disguised as a mandolin club, met in the inn Zum Kanonenkreuz in Karolinenthal. Max Brod sometimes came with me to the meetings, though he had little sympathy with them. . . . For me they were a very serious matter. I followed in the footsteps of Ravachol. They led me later to Erich Mühsam, Arthur Holitscher, and the Viennese anarchist Rudolf Gassman . . . they all attempted to realize the happiness of mankind without the aid of divine grace. But . . . I could not march shoulder to shoulder with them for long."[20] However, most commentators agree that this second version is less credible than the first, not only because of its mysterious origin (papers lost and found again) but also because of the factual error it contains: Max Brod has stated that he never went with his friend to the anarchist clubs, and also knew nothing about Kafka's participation in the activities of the Prague libertarian socialists.[21]

According to these different reports, Kafka stopped going to anarchist meetings after 1912. Why? In a book he published in 1965, Janouch counters the "totally false" claim that "Kafka lost interest in the anarchists in 1910–11 as a result of the trials against the Czech antimilitarists." Such a claim, he insists, could only be made by those who never understood Kafka's personality and his "complete engagement for humanity." In his view, if Kafka stopped going to the meetings, it was because of the dictatorial power exercised over the anarchist milieu by a certain Vohryzek—a man that turned out to be an agent of the police. (This was discovered after the opening of the imperial archives in 1918.) He adds that, even if he was disappointed by the amateurism of the Prague anarchists, Kafka did not cut his ties with the members of these clubs because he "admired their struggle to give a meaning to life, even if the means at their disposal were insufficient."[22] As in the case of the aforementioned texts by Janouch, it is hard to distinguish between authentic memories and later additions.

To these three known reports one can add a fourth, apparently unknown to all the biographers and commentators. In an article called "Kafka as a Young Man," published in a small North American literary review, Leopold B. Kreitner (1892–1969)—an alumnus of the gymnasium where Kafka studied—claims to have met with him frequently during the years 1912–1914. According to Kreitner, during his final years at the university and the decisive years that followed, Kafka's politics and philosophy turned toward "a sort of socialist cosmopolitanism, abhorring any nationalism." Kreitner remembers having heard from Jaroslav Hasek and Karel Toman (the anarchist poet) that Kafka "was a frequent, but not a regular visitor" at the meetings of the Young People's Club, a group of Czech writers and poets that met in the U Brejsku hotel, where they held animated discussions on literature, art, philosophy, and politics "in the direction of socio-anarchism."[23]

There are therefore four witnesses—to which one should add the fifth, anonymous one, that confirmed Kacha's reports to Brod—who describe, in more of less detail, the links between Kafka and the Prague milieu of socialist libertarianism.[24]

It's probable that some of these reports contain inaccuracies and distortions. Klaus Wagenbach himself admits, in the case of Mares, that "some details may be wrong" or at least "exaggerated." And according to Max Brod, Mares, like many other witnesses who knew Kafka, "tends to exaggerate," especially when claiming a friendship with the author. As for Janouch, the first version of his memoirs gives the impression of "authenticity and credibility" because they "present the distinctive style of Kafka's conversation," but the second seems to him much less trustworthy.[25] But it's one thing to note the contradictions and exaggerations in these documents and quite another to reject them totally, by calling the links between Kafka and the Czech anarchists "a pure fabrication." Yet this is the attitude of a few specialists such as Eduard Goldstücker, Hartmut Binder, Ritchie Robertson, and

Ernst Pawel. The first is a Czech Communist literary critic, and the three others are authors of Kafka biographies of an indisputable value. Their attempt to deny the anarchist episode in Kafka's life deserves to be discussed in detail, because it has obvious political implications.

According to Eduard Goldstücker—well known for his effort to "rehabilitate" Kafka in Czechoslovakia during the 1960s—the recollections of Mares republished by Wagenbach "belong to the realm of fiction." His central argument is that it is inconceivable that revolutionaries who were anarcho-communists would have accepted the presence at their meetings of "a man whom they did not know" and who, on top of that, "always remained silent." But what Goldstücker seems to forget is that Kafka, far from being "unknown," was, on the contrary, well known to two of the principal organizers of these meetings: Michal Kacha and Michal Mares (as well as to other participants such as Rudolf Illowy, his former classmate at the gymnasium). Still— somewhat in contradiction to what he said before—Goldstücker ends up admitting that Kafka sometimes participated in anarchist activities, but only for "a few meetings" and not for many years, as Mares claimed. Since Mares himself mentions only five meetings, it's hard to see why Goldstücker so categorically rejects his report.[26]

It's Hartmut Binder, the author of a detailed and very erudite biography of Kafka, who most energetically develops the thesis that the ties between Kafka and the Prague anarchist circles are a "legend" that belongs to "the realms of the imagination." He accuses Klaus Wagenbach of having used sources such as Kacha, Mares, and Janouch "to serve his own ideology," which, however, "lack credibility or even represent deliberate falsifications."[27]

This line of reasoning fails to explain why the three reports he describes as "unreliable" coincide in their affirmation of ties between Kafka and the anarchists; nor does it explain why we don't find other "fictive" reports about Kafka's repeated participation in Zionist, Communist, or social-democratic meetings. It's hard to understand— absent an anarchist conspiracy—why the so-called falsifications all point in one direction. All the more so because, in addition to the three reports known to critics, there is the fourth by Leopold Kreitner that Binder (and others) doesn't seem to be aware of.

However, let's look more closely at the arguments put forth by Binder, whose attack on Wagenbach is not without an "ideological" motivation. According to him, "The simple fact that Brod didn't learn of these supposed activities from the former member of the anarchist movement Michal Kacha until many years after Kafka's death . . . argues against the credibility of this information. It's almost unimaginable that Brod, who took two vacations with Kafka at this time and who saw him almost daily . . . would have been unaware of his best friend's interest in the anarchist movement."[28] Perhaps, but if it's really "almost unimaginable" (though the "almost" seems to leave some room for doubt), why is it that Max Brod himself considered this information totally reliable, since he mentions it in his novel *Stefan Rott* as well as in his biography of his friend? Another of Binder's arguments is no more convincing: "To be listening in a smoky beer joint to the political discussions of a group acting outside the limits of the law is an unimaginable situation for someone of Kafka's personality."[29] And yet Max Brod, who knew Kafka rather well, did not find anything strange in the situation . . . in fact, nothing in Kafka's oeuvre suggests that he had a superstitious respect for legality! In a final attempt to discredit the reports of Michal Mares, Binder refers to one of Kafka's letters to Milena in 1922, where he refers to Mares as someone he knew only slightly. He then goes on to say: "Kafka expressly emphasizes that his relationship to Mares is only that of a passing street acquaintance (*Gassenbekanntschaft*). This is the clearest indication that Kafka never participated in any anarchist meeting."[30] The least one can say is that the link between this premise and the conclusion is not very clear! All one can deduce from Kafka's letter to Milena is that Mares, in his report of 1946, probably exaggerated his friendship with Kafka; but there is no contradiction between their casual relations and Kafka's participation in anarchist meetings along with the young Mares, among others. Even if their relations were limited to meetings in the street (Kafka's house was near Mares's place of work), this wouldn't have prevented Mares from giving him tracts and invitations to meetings and protest demonstrations, and from noticing his presence in some of these activities; nor would it have prevented him from making Kafka a present of Kropotkin's book. In a September 1922 letter to Milena, Kafka refers to a "charming letter" (*reizenden Brief*) he received from Mares, and to a "very good" book of poetry that the latter gave him, *Policejni stara* (*Police Patrols*).[31]

As a material proof of his connections with Kafka, Mares is in possession of a postcard sent by the author, dated December 9, 1910. He claims to have received many letters from his friend that disappeared during the numerous official searches that he was subjected to in this period—a claim that is impossible to substantiate. Binder takes note of the existence of this document but, seeing that the postcard is addressed to "Josef Mares" (and not Michal), he thinks he has found yet another proof of the "fictions" of the witness: it would seem impossible that, a whole year after having met Mares and gone with him to several evening events at the Klub Mladych, Kafka "wouldn't even know his first name." However, this argument is fallible, for the simple reason that, according to the German editors of the correspondence between Kafka and Milena, Mares's first name was not Michal . . . but Josef.[32]

As for Janouch, Binder rejects the 1968 version of his memoir as pure invention, though the reference to anarchists in the 1951 version seems "possibly based on a real memory." At the same time he reduces its importance by associating it with the passage from the letter to Milena that describes the poet Michal Mares as a "street acquaintance." However, in the conversation reported by Janouch, Kafka is not talking about someone he met in the street but of "anarchists" in the plural, who are described as "nice and friendly." This leads one to suppose that Mares is far from being the only militant libertarian socialist whom Kafka knew.[33]

In general, Binder's discussion on this subject leaves one with the painful impression that he is waging a deliberate and systematic offensive in order to clear Kafka's image from the black stain (from the perspective of a conservative political stance) that would result from his participation in meetings organized by Prague anarchists.

A few years later, in an otherwise interesting biography, Ernst Pawel seems to defend the same ideas as Binder: he wants to "bury one of the great myths" that have attached themselves to Kafka, namely "the legend that Kafka was a co-conspirator at the heart of the Czech anarchist Klub Mladych." He attributes this legend to "imaginative reminiscences of the ex-anarchist Michal Mares," who, in his 1946 memoir, describes Kafka "as a friend and comrade who participated in anarchist meetings and demonstrations." Mares's story, "subsequently embroidered by Gustav Janouch, found its way into several Kafka biographies, from which he emerged as a youthful conspirator and fellow-traveler of the Czech libertarian socialist movement. The account, however, is wholly inconsistent with everything known about his life, his friends, and his character . . . he would scarcely have been willing or able to conceal his involvement from the close friends with whom he had almost daily contact."[34]

The "legend" is easy to disprove because it doesn't correspond to any claims made by the sources I have mentioned: neither Kacha (whom Pawel does not mention), nor Mares, nor Janouch—or even Wagenbach—ever claimed that "Kafka was a conspirator at the heart of an anarchist group." Mares explicitly insists on the fact that Kafka was not the member of any organization. Besides, it's not a question of "conspiracy" but of participation in meetings that were, for the most part, open to the public. As for "hiding his engagement from his intimate friends"—that is to say, Max Brod—I have already demonstrated the inanity of such a remark.

Ernst Pawel supplies one more argument in support of his thesis: it is "inconceivable for a quasi-government employee . . . to have escaped the attention of the ubiquitous police informers, who regularly accounted for a sizeable portion of the audience. Yet the files of a police department . . . contain not a single reference to Kafka."[35] It's an interesting observation, but the absence of a name in police archives has never in itself been a proof of nonparticipation. And in addition, it is improbable that the police knew the names of all those who went to public meetings organized by the different anarchist clubs: they were interested in the "leaders" and directors of these organizations, not in those who listened in silence.

However, Pawel differs from Binder in his willingness to recognize the facts suggested by these witnesses, albeit in attenuated form: "The truth is more prosaic. Kafka did indeed know Mares . . . and may well have attended a few public meetings or demonstrations as an interested observer. His own socialist leanings are attested to by Bergmann and Brod. . . . In later years, he also seems to have been intrigued by the non-violent philosophical anarchism of Kropotkin and Alexander Herzen."[36] We are not far from the conclusions drawn by Wagenbach.

Let's consider now the point of view of Ritchie Robinson, the author of a remarkable essay on the life and works of the Prague Jewish writer. According to him, the information furnished by Kacha and Mares should be "treated with skepticism." Most of his arguments are borrowed from Goldstücker and Binder: how could a group that meets secretly accept a silent visitor, "who, for all they knew, might have been a spy?" How is it possible that Brod knew nothing of his friend's participation in these meetings? How can one trust the reports of Mares, with whom he had not more than a "nodding acquaintance?" In sum, for all these reasons "Kafka's attendance at anarchist meetings looks very like a legend."[37] There is no point dealing with these objections since I have already shown them to be groundless.

What is new and interesting in Robertson's book is the attempt to propose an alternative interpretation of Kafka's political ideas: neither socialist nor anarchist but romantic—they are evidence, he says, of a romantic anticapitalism that is neither right nor left.[38] However, if romantic anticapitalism underlies some forms of conservative as well as revolutionary thinking (and in this sense really does avoid the traditional division between left and right), it is nonetheless true that the romantic authors situate themselves distinctly at one of two poles: reactionary romanticism or revolutionary romanticism.[39]

In fact, anarchism, antiauthoritarian socialism, and anarcho-syndicalism are paradigmatic examples of "leftist romantic anticapitalism." Therefore, to call Kafka's thinking romantic—which seems quite pertinent to me—in no way excludes the idea that he could be "on the left," and inspired by a romantic socialism with libertarian tendencies. As with all romantics, his criticism of modern civilization is tinged with nostalgia for the past—represented in his eyes by the Yiddish of the Jewish communities of Eastern Europe. He shares with them a suspicion of the ideology of progress and of the comfortable view that the history of modern civilization is that of an uninterrupted and irreversible march toward more enlightenment, freedom, and prosperity. In one of his aphorisms one finds the following cryptic remark: "Believing in progress does not mean believing that any progress has yet been made. That is not the sort of belief that indicates real faith (*Glauben*)."[40] Nevertheless, this opinion does not lead him, like the right-wing romantics, to nostalgic positions; rather he draws revolutionary conclusions, as can be seen in another aphorism: "The revolutionary spiritual movements that declare all former things worthless are in the right, for nothing has yet happened."[41]

The hypothesis, which has been suggested by the four witnesses, that Kafka was interested in anarchist ideas, is all the more credible in that it is corroborated by many references from his personal writings. For example, in a letter to Max Brod dated November 1917, he expresses his enthusiasm for the project of a periodical, *Blätter der Bekämpfung des Machtwillens* (*Papers for Fighting against the Will to Power*) proposed by the Freudian anarchist Otto Gross.[42] And above all, in his diaries one finds this categorical imperative: "Do not forget Kropotkin!"[43]

It's of course impossible to know what this exclamation refers to, but we can at least try to determine which of Kropotkin's works is in question. Quite probably—according to the editors of the diaries—it is the German edition of the *Memoirs of a Revolutionist* (1887), which, according to Brod, was one of Kafka's favorite books. Why was he so interested in the life of this Russian prince who became a revolutionary anarcho-communist? In addition to Kropotkin's moving accounts of his peripatetic and nomadic cosmopolitan life, the struggles, incarcerations, and escapes of a libertarian thinker who dreamed of the "suppression of all governments," as well as the courage and determination of a man who was able to break his ties with his own class to join the ranks of the oppressed, what could have attracted him to these memoirs? I can risk a hypothesis based on what we know of Kafka's personal preoccupations: one of the main themes in Kropotkin's book is the son's struggle against "the despotism of the fathers," defenders of serfdom. The young prince himself suffered from his father's authoritarianism, and his sympathy went out to the servants and serfs who were subjected to the brutality and arbitrariness of the head of the family. He therefore (to paraphrase Kafka in "Letter to My Father") "took sides with the serfs" and solemnly swore: "I will never be like him!"[44]

According to Kropotkin, it's the revolt of the young from the leisure classes against "domestic slavery"—which combines paternal despotism and "the hypocritical submissiveness by women, sons, and daughters"—that led them to criticize the existing state of things and to become "nihilists," or sworn adversaries of the czarist autocracy and of serfdom. In almost all rich families, he writes, there is a determined struggle going on between the fathers and the sons and daughters who want to defend their right to live according to their own ideals.[45] It seems to me that it's this intimate connection between the rebellion against the "domestic yoke" and against the state that interested the Prague author, rather than the particulars involved with the fights between federalists and centralists during the First International, or the syndicalist activities of watchmakers from the Jura.[46]

According to Brod, one finds the same leitmotiv in another of Kafka's favorite books: *My Past and Thoughts: The Memoirs of Alexander Herzen*, which he mentions several times in his diaries. According to

Isaiah Berlin, one can consider this great Russian nineteenth-century thinker as a semianarchist socialist who, above all in his youth, was close to Proudhon and Bakunin, about whom he writes admiringly in several chapters of his memoirs.[47] There too, the importance of the confrontation between paternal tyranny and son's rebellious vocation is striking. Some passages in Herzen's memoirs recall, almost word for word, paragraphs from the "Letter to My Father": "Mockery, irony and cold, caustic, utter contempt—these were the tools he wielded like an artist, employing them equally against us and against the servants. . . . Until I went to prison I was actually estranged from my father and joined with the maids and men-servants in waging a little war against him." Without actually being an anarchist, Herzen asked himself *"whether rational consciousness and moral independence are compatible with life in a State."*[48]

Kafka had also become aware of the German Jewish socialist Arthur Holitscher (1869–1941), whose 1912 *Amerika heute und morgen* (*America Today and Tomorrow*) became one of the principal sources for his novel *The Man Who Disappeared* (*America*). In describing his travel impressions in North America, the author is open about his sympathy for the anarcho-syndicalists of the Industrial Workers of the World (IWW), and in particular for William Haywood and Emma Goldman, whose radicalism and combativeness he contrasts with the futility of the "academic socialism" of the social-democratic leaders, lost in the labyrinthine "mills of parliamentary compromise" (*Kompromissmühle*).[49] Holitscher published his autobiography, *Lebensgeschichte eines Rebellen* (*Life Story of a Rebel*), in 1924, and Kafka mentions in his correspondence that he read it in March. In this work, Holitscher explains his rebellion against his bourgeois parents—who opposed his literary activities—his attraction to socialism and, later, to anarchism (Ravachol, Reclus, Jean Grave, Kropotkin).[50]

Kafka's interest was not limited to the autobiographies of anarchist authors. He was also interested in other trajectories, for instance in the memoirs of socialist women who had dedicated their lives to female emancipation, like Lily Braun—to whom I will return—and

Malwida von Meyseburg, a revolutionary democrat with ties to socialism, the friend of Garibaldi and Mazzini, and the governess to
Mazzini's children. This veteran of 1848 had taken refuge in London
and had decided early on in her life to "liberate herself from the authority of the family" in order to follow her "personal convictions"
and to fight for women's rights.[51]

We can conclude this short reminder of the libertarian socialist
readings of Kafka by mentioning an author that he cites in his diaries on two occasions: the poet and Czech author Franz Sramek,
who was an active participant in Prague anarchist circles.[52] Kafka's
library included a copy of *Flammen* (*Flames*), a volume of anarchist
and antimilitarist poems by Sramek, translated into German from
Czech by his friend Otto Pick and introduced by Hermann Bahr,
who describes the author as a revolutionary syndicalist and disciple
of Georges Sorel.[53]

Without "forgetting Kropotkin," Kafka stopped going to anarchist
meetings after 1913, while keeping his sympathy for them (at least,
this is what Janouch's notes suggest). His attention is more and more
engaged by Judaism, and to a certain extent Zionism. Among other
reasons, he was attracted by the social experiments of the rural col-
lectivities founded by the Jewish pioneers (*haloutzim*) in Palestine:
the kibbutzim. Felix Weltsch quotes Dora Dymant as saying: "Each
time he had the opportunity, he asked people he met about Palestine.
He was particularly interested by the pioneer movement—*Haloutz*."
Janouch also reports Kafka as saying, "I have dreamed of going as a
farm laborer or an artisan to Palestine."[54] This interest is not necessarily incompatible with his earlier inclinations, in the sense that the
kibbutzim movement was inspired in large part by the antiauthoritarian socialist ideas of Kropotkin, Gustav Landauer, and Martin Buber—at least, from the early twentieth century until the mid-1920s,
when Marxism became more influential. According to the historian
of anarchism Jean-Marc Izrine, "From the early twentieth century,
the humanist ideas and the anarcho-communist doctrine of Pyotr
Kropotkin seduced the pioneers of the kibbutzim movement. The

first *kvutzots* put those ideas into practice. . . . The antiauthoritarian obedience that took its cues from Bakunin and Kropotkin influenced the self-governing structure of the kibbutzim."[55]

His interest in the kibbutz shows that, despite his fierce individualism, Kafka was not at all hostile to collectivist experiences. One need only look at the curious document titled "Brotherhood of Poor Workers" (1918), which seems close to the model of Jewish communes in Palestine, at once because of its ascetic collectivism ("bread, water, dates"), its governance by a "Labor Council," and the radical absence of any private property. Many commentators have noted the presence, in this project, of the ideal of the "Jewish agrarian worker" developed in *Selbstwehr*, the periodical published by Kafka's Zionist friends, and of Tolstoy's and Kropotkin's anarchist collectivism. Hartmut Binder calls attention to the affinity between Kafka's utopian project and the ideas of the Zionist leader A. D. Gordon, a believer in the redemption of Jews through manual labor. It even appears that Kafka may have met Gordon during the Socialist Zionist Congress Hapoel Hatzaïr in Prague in 1920. Martin Buber also participated and gave a moving commemoration of Gustav Landauer, who had been assassinated the previous year. Still, it seems to me that Binder is mistaken in denying that Kafka's project had any socialist character; he describes it as "a professional expression of Jewish nationalism." However, the word "Jew" appears nowhere in this document, which proposes a workers' collective without any national or religious identity. In fact, this project of a "brotherhood of poor workers" is universal in its scope, surpassing the Jewish context that probably inspired it. It even fascinated André Breton, who, addressing the Rassemblement démocratique révolutionnaire (Assembly of Democratic Revolutionaries), or RDR, in 1948, called it a model of intellectual activity.[56] That said, it is not a question here of a utopian project for a new society—the state as well as capital are still present—but of a collectivist social experience within the framework of existing society.

In searching for the signs of Kafka's interest in libertarian socialist ideas, I am not trying to demonstrate a pretended "influence" of the Prague anarchists—or of Kropotkin—on his writings. On the contrary, he himself, *on account of his own experiences and his antiauthoritarian sensibility*, sought out these milieus for several years and chose to read some of their writings. Nothing would be more mistaken than to believe that he wanted to transcribe his sympathies into his literary works. If there is a "family resemblance" between the one and the other, it is because both are based on something fundamental, his existential attitude, an essential character trait, a way of relating to the world (*Sitz im Leben*). He defined this trait himself—in a sort of inflexible hardness, a remorseless sincerity—in his letter to Felice Bauer on October 19, 1916: "Having as a rule depended on others, I have an infinite longing for independence, self-reliance, freedom in all directions. . . . Any relationship not created by myself . . . is worthless; it hinders my movements. I hate it, or come near to hating it."[57] *An infinite longing for independence, self-reliance, freedom in all directions*: it would be impossible to define more accurately the red thread that runs through Kafka's life and works—especially the period from 1912 on—and gives them an extraordinary coherence, despite their tragic incompleteness.

This antiauthoritarian ethos is expressed in different situations that lie at the heart of his principal literary works, but above all in the radical critique of the obsessive and anxiety-producing face of nonliberty: authoritarianism. As Breton said so well about Kafka, "There is no writing that militates as strongly against the acceptance, by the thinking person, of a sovereign external principle."[58]

Still, libertarian socialist utopianism as such does not appear anywhere in his novels and stories: it exists only as a negative, as the critique of a world completely deprived of liberty, at the mercy of the absurd and arbitrary logic of an all-powerful "apparatus." As Franz Baumer observes, "The will to freedom that motivates Kafka's characters is the revolutionary aspect of his thinking and his writing: it is always a question of absolute freedom."[59] Once again, at issue is not any sort of *political doctrine*, but a *state of mind* and a *critical sensibility*—whose main weapon is *irony and humor*—that *black humor* that Breton called *"the superior revolt of the mind."*[60]

This kind of "critical" interpretation is of course in flagrant contradiction with many metaphysical readings that claim that Kafka's novels demonstrate a resignation before the eternal "human condition." Theodor Adorno put this kind of argument to rest in a remarkable formulation: "His work has the tone of the extreme left; to level it down to the 'universally human' is to falsify it conformistically."[61] This polemical remark deserves a comment. Adorno is not speaking of a message, a doctrine, or a thesis, but of a *tonality*, in the musical sense of the term. It's unlikely that Adorno knew of the reports of Kafka's libertarian socialist sympathies. It's rather through an immanent reading of the literary texts that he arrived at this conclusion. His statement about the "extreme left" tone (a term that Adorno rarely used) of Kafka's works has several implications. First of all, it means that the works' problematics are not metaphysical but historical: they affect modern (bourgeois) society. Second, sccording to Adorno, this society, or civilization, is portrayed by Kafka in a radically critical manner, as "infernal"; and finally, this radical critique encompasses the idea of the abolition of the existing social order and its replacement by a liberated humanity ("redemption").[62]

To summarize, even without knowing about Kafka's contacts with the Prague anarchist circles, one can easily grasp the subversive and antiauthoritarian dimension of his oeuvre by an attentive and sensitive reading of his texts. The biographical documents only confirm what is revealed by an "internal" analysis of the works.[63]

CHAPTER 2

TYRANNIES, FROM PATRIARCHAL AUTOCRACY TO IMPERSONAL APPARATUSES

Kafka was far from being an "anarchist," but antiauthoritarianism—of a romantic and libertarian socialist quality—runs through his writings, *in a growing universalization and increasingly abstract representation of power*: from paternal and personal authority toward administrative and anonymous authority. As Elias Canetti observes: "Of all writers, Kafka is the greatest expert on power. He experienced it in all its aspects, and he gave shape to this experience."[1]

But what kind of power is this? In an illuminating commentary, Adorno suggests that most of Kafka's literary output is "a reaction to unlimited power." He goes on to say: "To this power, that of the raging patriarch, Benjamin gave the name 'parasitic': it lives off the lives it oppresses."[2] The first statement does in fact apply to most of Kafka's writings, which consist of a critical, ironic, and anxious reaction against the multiple manifestations of despotic and limitless power. The second comment applies essentially to "The Judgement," *The Metamorphosis*, and in part to *The Man Who Disappeared* (*America*), whose heroes are the victims of "raging patriarchs." It's not by accident that Kafka thought of publishing the two novellas along with the first chapter ("The Stoker") of his novel, with the title *The Sons* (*Die Söhne*).

The first of these patriarchs is of course the father, Hermann Kafka. In the impressive 1919 document "Letter to My Father"—one of the essential keys to understanding the personality of the author— Franz complains about Hermann's "despotic character," comparing him several times to a "tyrant"[3] and "autocrat," and about the "dreadful trial in which we [Kafka and his sister Ottla] and you are entangled"; a "trial in which you claim always to be the judge."[4] He defines his own childhood situation as that of "the slave" living "under laws invented solely for my life" confronted with a world in which "you lived, infinitely far from me, busy ruling, giving commands and being angry when they weren't followed."[5] The father's "authoritarian character" (*herrisches Temperament*) is evidenced by the fact that he uses any method—"abuse, threats, irony, a mocking laugh"—to more completely exercise his domination and to use fear to entirely subject his son to his will.[6] This domination is literally without limits; in a startling image, Kafka extends the patriarchal authority and body into space: "Sometimes I imagine the map of the world laid out and you stretched across it. And all that is left for my life are the areas you don't cover or can't reach."[7] In the end, it's in the realm of literature that Franz managed to find a refuge at the farthest remove from the empire of the father.[8]

The same set of problems returns in an almost obsessive fashion in the *Diaries*. In a 1911 entry, Franz goes so far as to speak of his "hatred" of Hermann, who not only covered him with reproaches but also insulted his friends Max Brod—whom he calls "a crazy hothead" (*meschuggener ritoch*)—and Isaac Löwy—whom he compares to a dog that brings fleas into the house.[9] The confrontation with paternal authority will be a permanent dimension of his identity, as is evidenced by the following late entry on December 2, 1921, which appears to condense in a remarkable way the writer's family "battleground": "This thought lately, that as a little child I had been defeated by my father and because of ambition have never been able to quit the battlefield all these years despite the perpetual defeats I suffer."[10]

This conflict is not only psychological and oedipal; it has a larger historical context: on the one hand, the cultural politics of the Austro-Hungarian Empire—the "Cacania" described so well by Musil—that appears to cement into the same authoritarian paternalism all the representatives of power, from the Kaiser himself to the pater familias, passing through the heads of ministries, prefects, and other directors of establishments; and on the other, a whole generation of young Jewish intellectuals born at the end of the nineteenth century, attracted to a romantic vision of the world, and passionately aspiring to a life dedicated to art, culture, or revolution. They would radically break with the generation of their bourgeois parents, who were merchants, industrialists, or bankers, moderate liberal or assimilated Germans. But in Franz's case the conflict is exacerbated by Hermann's authoritarianism and his hostility to his son's literary activities.[11] For him, there is a clear connection between the "limitless power" of the father, the despotic authority of the "raging patriarch" (Adorno's term), and tyranny as a political system. In the "Letter to My Father" he remarks that both follow the same logic: "You became for me that puzzle which belongs to all tyrants: the law lay in your person and not in your wisdom."[12] And commenting on his father's brutal, unjust, and arbitrary behavior toward the employees of the family business, he writes: "The place upset me—it reminded me of my relationship with you . . . therefore I belonged essentially to the workers' party."[13]

Such are the deeply personal roots of his affinity with the Prague libertarian socialists, and of the antiauthoritarian sensibility of his novels and short stories. His statement about his "siding with the staff" is no accident. As Elias Canetti observes, "From the beginning, Kafka sides with the humiliated."[14] Several entries in the *Diaries* mention his sympathy for the workers, for instance his description of the condition of the female workers in the family-owned asbestos factory: "The girls, in their unbearably dirty and untidy clothes, their hair disheveled as if they had just got up, the expressions on their faces fixed by the incessant noise of the transmission belts and by the individual machines . . . they aren't treated as people, you don't greet them, you don't apologize if you bump into them . . . they are at the mercy of the pettiest power."[15]

Many of his texts and literary drafts describe the disdainful, snobbish, and brutal behavior of "those on high." For example, in the story of Bauz (included in the *Diaries*), the director of the insurance company Progress says to a lowly unemployed man who comes to ask for a job as attendant for the company: "Trembling like that won't do any good. I have no authority to hand out favors . . . and now I'm telling you for the last time. Go along and don't take up any more of my time"—a pronouncement that is accompanied by a rap of the table, while the man is led out of the director's office by the attendants.[16] Or again the short text "The new light fixtures," where men from the administration treat the perfectly legitimate request by a delegation of miners for new light fixtures with ironic disdain: "You go and tell the men down there: you'll never stop until your tunnels have become a salon and, to top it off, until you die wearing polished shoes . . . get out of here!" Even in his work in the Workingmen's Accident Insurance Company, Kafka allowed himself, from time to time, to let his preferences show—for instance in this report on the work accidents in the civilian construction industry, where he regrets "the absence of the working-class voice (*Arbeiterschaft*) in the debate over security measures," a lack that he attributes to "insufficient organization among the workers," especially in the small businesses—a remark that would seem to come from the pen of a trade unionist rather than from the undersecretary of the Workingmen's Accident Insurance Company.[17]

Let us return once more to the "Letter to My Father," since this document offers the clearest understanding of the empathy Kafka felt for other young victims of paternal authoritarianism, such as Otto Gross. Interned in a psychiatric hospital on his father's orders in 1913, the Freudian anarchist Otto Gross owed his liberation entirely to a press campaign mounted by expressionist writers. Inspired by Nietzsche, Freud, and Max Stirner, he attacked, in his

writings, the will to power, patriarchy, and the principle of authority in the family as well as in society. At the law school Kafka had
been the student of Otto's father, Hans Gross, author of a manual for
magistrates, correctional officers, and constables and a fierce pro-
ponent of the deportation of "degenerate" individuals, such as "the
lazy, the eternally discontented and the subversives." Kafka met the
son during a train trip in July 1917; shortly thereafter, during a meeting in Prague, Otto Gross proposed to publish, with Werfel and
Kafka, a journal called *Papers for the Struggle Against the Will to
Power* (*Blätter zur Bekämpfung des Machtwillens*). In a letter to Brod
on November 14 of the same year, Kafka expresses great interest for
the project.[18] It would seem that Otto Gross personifies for him the
convergence of the revolt against paternal tyranny and the (anarchist) resistance to any institutional authority.

The Swiss writer Max Pulver, who met Kafka in 1917, provides a
fascinating account that highlights the intimate connection between
these two aspects in the character and personality of his interlocutor:
"In the trial he led against the world, he implicated not only his father,
but all fathers, the world of fathers and authority figures . . . he exercised a strange attraction through his insubordination, his air of se-
crecy, and his contempt for any kind of authority—the attraction of
intransigence, its seductive quality." Rebellion, intransigence, refusal
of the father's authority and of any form of authority: this is an apt
and powerful characterization of the *state of mind* in which Kafka
composed a good part of his writings.

Consider "The Judgment" of 1912. In this short story that constitutes a new departure in his literary oeuvre and anticipates his principal works, Kafka focuses on the authority of the father. A young
businessman, George Bendemann, visits his aging father, who, under
false pretexts—his son's alleged inattention toward a friend who has
left for Russia—condemns his son to death by drowning. This extraordinarily cruel novella is one of the rare writings of Kafka in
which the hero entirely and uncomplainingly submits to the authoritarian judgment (by throwing himself in the river).[19] One could sum-

marize the ineluctable logic at the base of this story as follows: it's impossible to escape patriarchal tyranny, yet blind obedience to it is a kind of suicide.

The conventional interpretation of this novella asserts that the son is guilty—because he is egotistical, because he tended to neglect his progenitor, and so on. The logic of this kind of reading—which we will also find in the secondary literature about *The Trial*—is implacable: because the father accuses him, and because the son accepts the verdict and carries out the sentence, he must be guilty of something . . . whereas this completely misses the essential point: the brutal injustice and total arbitrariness of the "raging patriarch."[20]

Commenting on this text, Walter Benjamin observes: the father "sentences his son to death by drowning. The father is the one who punishes; he is drawn to guilt, just as the court officials are. There is much to indicate that the world of officials and the world of fathers are the same to Kafka."[21] Milan Kundera proposes an analogous hypothesis. Comparing "The Judgment" and *The Trial*, he comments: "The resemblance between the two accusations, establishments of guilt and executions, betrays the continuity that connects intimate family 'totalitarianism' to that of Kafka's grand vision."[22] This continuity is essential if one wants to understand the atmosphere of the great novels, though these undoubtedly contain a new element absent from "The Judgment": the increasingly anonymous, hierarchical, opaque, and distant character of power. It's no longer the father who punishes and/or kills; it's the administrative apparatus.

One should stress once again at this point that neither in this short story nor in the writings that followed did Kafka wish to transmit any sort of "message." He wrote as inspiration led him, without a preestablished "goal," and he was incapable of furnishing any sort of "explanation" once the work was completed. A letter to Felice dated June 2, 1913, is explicit on this point: "Can you discover any meaning in the "Judgment,"—some straightforward, coherent meaning that one could follow? I can't find any, nor can I explain anything in it."[23] Of course there is a lot of irony and self-irony in this affirmation, but it applies nonetheless not only to this novella, but also, in all probability, to the author's entire oeuvre. This does not disqualify attempts at explanation, but these are useless for positing an a priori intention of the author.

The Metamorphosis of 1912 is also a short story about the murderous power of the father. Changed into a gigantic insect (*Ungeziefer*), Gregor Samsa is threatened at every moment by attacks from his father. He is saved from the rage of the patriarch only by the mother who grabs the father and begs for her son's life.[24] Wounded, bruised, damned, and abandoned, he dies. It's the maid who takes charges of the "remains," sweeping them away with her broom: "You don't need to bother about how to get rid of the thing next door. It's been done already."[25] In order to understand this famous and terrifying fable about "family totalitarianism," it's useful to recall that Kafka, in the "Letter to My Father," complains that the latter considers him a "parasite" and an "insect" (*Ungeziefer*).[26] Of course, this dimension, while important, in no way exhausts the "meaning" of the story , which remains mysterious and, like any poetic work, "inexplicable." In any case, this was the writing that inspired Oskar Walzel in 1916 to coin the expression "logic of the marvelous."

The Man Who Disappeared (*America*) from 1913–1914 represents a transitional work from the point of view of forms of authoritarianism. The dominant personalities are paternal figures (Karl Rossman's father and his uncle Jacob), but also people who have come down in the world (Delamarche) and high administrators (the head maître d'hôtel and the porter of the Occidental Hotel). All of them embody an unendurable authoritarianism that will show itself in the novels and stories of the coming years: arbitrary opinions without any justification, whether moral, rational, or human; excessive and absurd demands placed on the victimized hero; injustice (the false assumption of guilt, considered indubitable and unquestioned); and a punishment in complete disproportion to the (nonexistent or trivial) transgression.

The one who obeys without resisting ends up becoming "a dog."

When one is always treated like a dog, says the oppressed Robinson, "One ends up thinking that one really is a dog." The young Karl Rossmann believes, nonetheless, that this happens only to those who let others do it to them; as for him, he obeys only his paternal figures (his father and his uncle) and tries to resist the others, even physically. The most heinous by far are the heads of the Occidental Hotel's administrative hierarchy, who embody the principle of authority. In refusing the conciliatory advances of the head cook, the maître d'hôtel cries out: "It's a matter of my authority, there's is a lot at stake, a boy like that will spoil the lot of them."[27] Their bureaucratic authoritarianism—which crushes little Karl situated at the very bottom on the enormous hierarchical ladder of servants—retains, nonetheless, an element of personal tyranny; it combines bureaucratic coldness with a cruel personal despotism that borders on sadism, as the head porter takes a sinister pleasure in brutalizing the young Rossmann.[28]

The symbol of this punitive authoritarianism appears in the first pages of the book: in an ironic twist, Kafka presents the Statue of Liberty in the New York harbor as wielding a sword, rather than the traditional torch.[29] In a world without liberty or justice, brute force and arbitrary power have absolute rule. The hero's sympathy goes out to the suffering victims of this society, to the stoker of the first chapter, a poor soul lost among the powerful, or to Therese's mother, impelled by hunger and misery to suicide. He finds friends and allies among the poor: Therese herself, the student worker, the inhabitants of the popular quarter who refuse to deliver him to the police— because, as Kafka writes, "Workmen don't side with officials."[30]

There is another indication of the extent to which some of the bureaucrats of *The Man Who Disappeared* (*America*) are linked to paternal authority: in the porters' lodge, the porters push objects off the counter that then have to be picked up by the exhausted messenger boys. Significantly, this is how Kafka describes his father's behavior toward his employees: "the way you would push goods you did not want to have mixed up with others, knocking them off the counter . . . and the assistant had to pick them up."[31]

The Man Who Disappeared (America) is without a doubt the novel that has the closest affinities with the Marxist critique of capitalist industrial society. This is particularly clear in the descriptions of the uncle's business and that of the Occidental Hotel as private enterprises that pitilessly exploit their employees. The communist literary journal *Kmen* perceived this and published a Czech translation by Milena Jesenska of the first chapter ("The Stoker") in 1920. Kafka had not read Marx, but he knew socialist writings that, in one way or another, were inspired by Marxism. Among the books he read at this time one finds the works of Holitscher as well as Lily Braun's autobiography. These have elements of the Marxist critique of worker exploitation and alienation. The same could be said for articles by Eduard Bernstein or Kurt Eisner appearing in the *Neue Rundschau* (to which Kafka subscribed) between 1909 and 1913.[32]

However, it seems to me that the criticism of American society that is sketched out in this novel, and in particular the power that modern technical apparatus exercise over human life, is inspired above all by the romanticist protest against modern bourgeois *Zivilisation* as expressed by the Bar Kochba circle of his Zionist friends—a protest that appears in their collection *Vom Judentum* of 1913 and that figures in Kafka's library. The disquieting descriptions of mechanized work in the novel are evidence of this. The employees of Rossman's uncle, the proprietor of a gigantic commercial enterprise—spend their days enclosed in telephone booths, indifferent to everything, their heads held in the grip of a steel band: only their fingers move, in a mechanical rhythm described as "inhuman regularity (*gleichmässig*) and rapidity."[33] In the same way, the "lift-boys" in the Occidental Hotel perform work that is harassing, exhausting, and monotonous (*einförmig*); they spend their time pushing buttons while remaining in total ignorance about the functioning of the machines. In the offices and streets the noise is all-pervasive: "The noise raced over the pavement and the roadway, changing direction each moment as though in a whirlwind, seeming not like a product of humanity but like an alien element."[34]

One could multiply the examples: the whole atmosphere of the book reveals the unrest and anxiety of individuals delivered to a pitiless world and a technical society that they cannot grasp. As Wilhelm Emrich observes, this work is "one of the must lucid criticisms of modern industrial society in the world. The economic mechanisms and secret psychology of this society and its satanic consequences are exposed without holding anything back." The world of the novel is dominated by the monotonous and circular return of the same, by the purely quantitative temporality of the clock.[35] The America of the novel is perceived as a *Zivilisation* without *Kultur*: neither art nor the mind seems to play a role any more, and the only book mentioned is a guide to commercial correspondence.[36] We know that one of the main sources for the novel was the 1912 book by the Jewish socialist Arthur Holitscher, *Amerika Heute und Morgen*, in which one finds a detailed description of the "inferno" represented by modern American civilization and a biting critique of Taylorism: "The specialization of work that results from mass production reduces the worker more and more to the level of a dead piece of machinery, to a wheel or cog functioning with precision and automatism."[37]

However, the authoritarian aspect of American civilization is much stronger in *Amerika* than in Holitscher's book: it's Kafka who brings out the omnipresence of domination in social relations. This difference is particularly apparent in Holitscher's chapter "Hotel Athenäum, Chautauqua." In this grand modern hotel there is an elevator boy—a high school student—exactly like Karl Rossmann in the Occidental Hotel. However, far from being oppressed, like Kafka's hero, by a pitiless bureaucratic hierarchy, he converses about Latin grammar with a rich hotel guest. Holitscher concludes that class differences are less pronounced in America than in Europe.[38]

Kafka's suspicion of modern technology no doubt also arises from his experience as an employee of the Workingmen's Accident Insurance Company: in the increasing number of work accidents—which he documented in detail with diagrams and illustrations in his professional reports—he witnessed the dark underside of the triumphant era of technological progress.[39] As Max Brod understood, his "professional experience" pushed him, once again, to take "the side of the workers" (as he said in the "Letter to His Father"), that is to say, the side of the accident victims: "His social conscience was greatly stirred when he saw workers crippled through neglect of safety precautions." To illustrate this point, he cites one of Kafka's remarks that seems inspired by anarchist ideas of direct action: "How modest these men are. . . . They come to us and beg. Instead of storming the institute and smashing it to pieces, they come and beg."[40]

Kafka's correspondence during this period also reveals his own feelings of anxiety in the face of the mechanization of the world: in a letter to Felice from January 10, 1913, he criticizes the "Parlograph" (Dictaphone): "A machine with its silent, serious demands strikes me as exercising a greater, more cruel compulsion (*grausamern Zwang*) on one's capacities than any human being. . . . He who dictates is master, but faced with a Parlograph he is degraded and becomes a factory worker whose brain has to serve a whirring machine."[41] A few years later, during a conversation with Janouch, he openly expresses his hostility to Taylorism, in a comment that takes on biblical resonance: "Such a violent outrage can only end in enslavement to evil. It is inevitable. Time, the noblest and most essential element in all creative work, is conscripted into the net of corrupt business interests. Thereby not only creative work, but man himself, who is its essential part, is polluted and humiliated. A Taylorized life is a terrible curse which will give rise only to hunger and misery instead of the intended wealth and profit."[42]

This moral and religious hostility to the "progress" of industrial capitalism, this typical romantic anxiety in the face of the nightmare of mechanized human life, is accompanied in Kafka by a nostalgia for the traditional community, the organic Gemeinschaft, that attracts him to the Yiddish culture (and language) of the Jews of Eastern Europe, to the projects of rural life in Palestine, as well as to (but more ambiguously) the romantic and cultural Zionism of his Prague friends. The Czech peasant community, living in peace and harmony with nature, also warrants his enthusiastic admiration: "General impression given one by peasants: noblemen who have escaped into agriculture, where they have arranged their work so wisely and humbly that it fits perfectly into everything and they are protected against all insecurity and worry until their blissful death. True dwellers on this earth."[43] It is startling to compare this idyllic and peaceful tableau to the description of the feverish pace of the port of New York, in the first chapter of *The Man Who Disappeared*: "An incessant motion, an unrest, transferred from the restless elements to the helpless humans and their works."[44]

Soon after he wrote *The Man Who Disappeared*, Kafka composed the short story "In the Penal Colony." Among all his writings, this is the one in which authority is presented in its most murderous and unjust guise. It is also one of the most remarkable for its unrestrained violence; even more than his other writings, it causes a perturbation of the contemplative relation between reader and text that, according to Adorno, constitutes a fundamental convergence between Kafka and surrealism: "His texts are designed so as not to sustain a constant distance between themselves and their victim (*Opfer*) but rather to agitate . . . [the reader's] feelings to a point where he fears that the narrative will shoot towards him like a locomotive in a three-dimensional film."[45]

One of the best commentaries on this important text is the review by Kurt Tucholsky in the *Weltbühne* of June 13, 1920, published on the occasion of the first printing of the work. He writes that this masterpiece, though presenting itself as a dream, has nothing of a dream's fuzziness: it's a dream that is "pitilessly hard, cruelly objective with a crystalline clarity" whose essential theme is servitude to power. And, he adds, "This power has no limits (*Diese Macht hat keine Schranken*)."[46]

Once again we find, in the novella "In the Penal Colony," the figures of traditional and personal power (of a patriarchal origin) with the two Commanders—the old one and the new one. But the role that these characters play is relatively limited and the expression of authority is displaced onto the impersonal execution machine. The strange functioning of this purely imaginary instrument, wholly invented by the author, largely contributes to the fascination of this literary creation.

It is hard, after 1945, to read this sinister narrative without thinking of the "death industries" of Nazism, and the extermination by perfected methods of millions of Jews and Romani. In the light of the experience of the Shoah, critics from Adorno to George Steiner have suggested that this is Kafka's most prophetic oeuvre. More recently, Enzo Traverso has suggested that "In the Penal Colony" appears to presage the anonymous massacres of the twentieth century, in which killing becomes a technical operation that is more and more subtracted from people's direct intervention. The "harrow" imagined by Kafka that inscribes the death sentence on the victim's skin calls to mind the tattooing of the inmates of Auschwitz, the indelible number that made them feel, as Primo Levi said, "their death sentence inscribed in their skin."[47] There is doubtless something prophetic in this short story. However, in order to understand this remarkable text, we need to investigate the models and the motivations that inspired Kafka in his own time. It seems to me that the writer deals here with three intimately associated forms of domination: the colonial, the military, and (more indirectly) the bureaucratic.

First, Kafka is referring to the reality of his era: *colonialism*, and in particular French colonialism. The officers and Commanders of the "Colony" are French; the lowly soldiers, the dockworkers, and the condemned victims are "indigenous" men who do not understand a word of French. The exact name of this "tropical" location is not specified. One can imagine that it is Devil's Island, where Captain Dreyfus was sent after his sentencing, but there was no indigenous population there.[48] Or perhaps it is New Caledonia, that French "penal colony" inhabited by Melanesians, to which the prisoners of the Paris Commune were deported—yet Kafka does not mention deportations, whether political or otherwise.[49] In fact, the island in the story seems more like an "ordinary" colony than a "penal colony." Why did he title it "In the Penal Colony" when there are no deported prisoners? The German term *Strafkolonie* suggests a possible answer, if we put the emphasis on punishment (*Strafe*): it would seem to be a colony in which the emphasis is put on the apparatus of punishment. Whatever the case may be, the characters are typical of any colonial regime: a white elite and an indigenous mass. This colonial background explains the extraordinary violence of domination that is much more direct and brutal here than in *The Man Who Disappeared* or, later, in *The Castle* and *The Trial*. This kind of critical vision of colonial power was rare, or nonexistent, in the literature of the times.[50]

The novella presents three distinct features of colonialism: first, an extreme cruelty, incarnated in the old Commander and by the officer. Their discourse has, for sure, a certain religious flavor, but it's a parody of religion, providing a transcendental justification for a sinister form of oppression.[51] Second, there is the more "humanitarian" cruelty of the new Commander, who considers abolishing the torture machine but who, in the meantime, allows it to continue functioning (although with more discretion than before). This "gentler" form of domination finds its humanitarian ritual in the distribution, by the Commander's wife and other women of the colonial elite, of sweets to the condemned. Finally, there is the more enlightened attitude of the traveler, a European repelled by the barbaric colonial methods of execution but who does nothing to stop the killing of the condemned native, and who, in the end, only takes a "private" position against this system of torture and that only after long hesitation. Admittedly this discreet opposition has definite consequences—discouraged, the officer takes the place of the condemned and has himself executed. As for the traveler, he flees by taking the first boat that is leaving the colony (no doubt for Europe), but not without having forcefully prevented the two natives—the soldier and the prisoner—from leaving as well.[52]

The colonized appear more as victims of domination than as autonomous subjects. This corresponds to reality, in an era when rebellion in the colonies was a rare occurrence. So it's all the more interesting that the condemned soldier, before submitting "like a dog," has a moment of legitimate revolt, in grabbing the whip from the officer who was lashing him. It's also interesting that, after the death of the officer (which appears to them as a kind of social revenge) the soldier and the prisoner become complicit and try to join together in fleeing the colony.

In addition to colonialism, the story takes a critical stance toward the *military institution*. Kafka is describing a monstrous revenge carried out by the insulted military authority. The poor soldier is condemned to death for lack of discipline and insulting behavior toward a superior. What is his "crime"? Having failed to accomplish an exaggerated and ridiculous task, and having been struck in the face by the officer's whip, he dared to rebel against authority with a cry of protest. Without any possibility of defending himself, and according to the judicial doctrine of the officers which proclaims that "guilt is never in doubt," the man is condemned to be executed by a torture machine that will slowly engrave onto his body (with transpiercing needles), "Honor thy superiors."[53]

The author's hostility toward military authoritarianism and the anxiety that it inspires in him finds a remarkable expression in this novella. As we saw, Kafka was close to the Prague milieu of anarchists and antimilitarists during the years 1909–1912. His affinity with their ideas is alluded to in a passage of the *Diaries*, on the occasion of a visit to Switzerland in 1911: "The impression foreign soldiers make on one of being out of the past. The absence of it in one's own. Anti-militarist argument."[54] Though the reasoning is somewhat enigmatic, the conclusion is perfectly clear: Kafka is looking into his travel impressions for arguments favorable to the combat against militarism.[55]

One can find the same antimilitarist sentiments in some of Kafka's literary fragments, as, for example, in this brief text: "There came two soldiers and seized me. I struggled, but they held firm. They conducted me to their master, an officer. How gay his uniform was! I said: 'What do you want with me, I am a civilian.' The officer smiled and said: 'You are a civilian, but that does not protect us from seizing you.

The army has power over everything' (*das Militär hat Gewalt über alles*)."[56] In these few lines one finds a condensed version of the insubordinate attitude of the narrator who tries in vain to defend his freedom; his ironic attitude toward the bright uniform of the officer; his refusal to recognize the authority of military personnel over his person; and the unequal relation between them and himself (the civilian uses the formal address, *Sie*, toward the officer, who responds with *Du*, a disrespectful familiar address). The officer, on the other hand, affirms in a threatening way the administrative—and in fact totalitarian—role of the army. It would be difficult to find a more concise, lively, and succinct expression of mistrust of military matters.

To come back to "In the Penal Colony," the principal character in this disturbing story is neither the officer—who functions at the same time as judge, executioner, and technician—nor the traveler, who observes the events with a critical eye, nor the prisoner, nor even, as has often been claimed, the Commander. It is the machine, the *apparatus*.

The whole narration turns around this lethal piece of engineering—its origin, its so-called automatic operation, and its meaning : one doesn't need to adjust it manually, for "it regulates itself automatically."[57] The protagonists of the drama play their roles around this central fact. The apparatus, whose every movement is calculated with precision, appears more and more like an end in itself. It is there not merely to execute a man; it's the man who is there for the machine, to supply a body on which the machine can write its aesthetic masterpiece, its bloody inscription accompanied with "lots and lots of flourishes around the script."[58] One finds here again—though expressed much more powerfully—the romantically inspired criticism, in *The Man Who Disappeared*, of the nefarious power of modern machinery. The officer himself is no more than a servant to the machine—and finally sacrifices himself to this insatiable Moloch. Her authority appears in its most alienating and reified guise, as an "objectified" mechanism.[59] A fetish created by humans, it is a thing that enslaves, dominates, and destroys them.

What specific "machine" of human sacrifice was Kafka thinking of? "In the Penal Colony" was written in October 1914, three months after the start of the First World War. For him, world war was an inhuman and murderous mechanism, a sort of blind and reified meshing of gears that operated outside of human control. But the image of war as "apparatus" also has a second and more immediate significance: it's an immense confrontation between killing machines. In a text he wrote in 1916—an appeal for a hospital for the victims of nervous diseases due to the war—Kafka is explicit: "This great war, which encompasses the sum total of human misery is also a war on the nervous system, more a war on the nervous system than any previous war. All too many people succumb to this war of nerves. Just as the intensive industrialization of the past decades of peace had attacked, affected, and caused disorders of the nervous systems of those engaged in industry more than ever before, so the enormously increased mechanization of present-day warfare presents the gravest dangers and disorders to the nervous system of fighting men."[60]

In associating the old Commander, the officer, and the apparatus, Kafka captured, with astonishing lucidity, a central characteristic of the First World War: the inextricable knot and intimate connection between the most archaic, retrograde, outmoded, patriarchal, pseudoreligious, and brutal authoritarianism, and the most modern, refined, exact, "calculated," "rational" technology. The whole was put into service for the most concrete and precise objective: the killing of human beings. Isn't what the writer has grasped here one of the possible developments of modern Western society and its instrumental rationality? A development that would show, in the course of the twentieth century, its immense potential for barbarism.

One can also suppose that the story's apparatus designates the modern bureaucratic state as such, and not only in its colonial or military character. To be sure, bureaucracy as such is not an engine of extermination, but Kafka, in his conversations with Janouch, did not shy away from comparing the bureaucrat to an executioner.[61]

To criticize the state as an inhuman and mechanical system is a tradition within romanticism, the source of the first expressions of this train of thought. Writing in 1797, the young Schelling already proclaimed that "every state necessarily treats free human beings as a system of interlocking mechanical wheels and gears (*mechanisches Räderwerk*).[62] Modern anarchism—Kropotkin!—is the heir to this romantic criticism, although one finds echoes even in the work of some German sociologists such as Alfred Weber. It's possible that Kafka was familiar with the latter's 1910 article on "the employee" from the *Neue Rundschau* (to which he subscribed), which describes bureaucracy as a "vast apparatus" (*Apparat*), a "dead mechanism" that exercises its domination on our entire existence.[63] I will come back to this.

There are numerous political or sociological works that criticize colonialism, militarism, or bureaucracy. What Kafka adds with the resources of literature is a singular imaginary universe that does not "reflect" reality but rather illuminates it with a new and incomparably powerful light.

How can we explain the transition from the stories that describe a limitless patriarchal power to the dramatization, in the novella "In the Penal Colony," of limitless power as an impersonal mechanism? Perhaps several factors played a role in this process of "depersonalization" and objectification of authority; yet it does not seem accidental to me that the decisive moment comes at the beginning of the First World War—a formidable manifestation of the power of state apparatuses and their murderous logic.

In the writings that followed, *The Trial* and *The Castle*, it's the impersonal and hierarchical (juridical or administrative) apparatus of the state that takes center stage. The conflict with paternal authority is not forgotten, but *aufgehoben* (suppressed/retained/transcended) in this new approach.

It has been Marxist dissident readers like Walter Benjamin, Bertolt Brecht, Theodor Adorno, Ernst Fischer, and Karel Kosik who were the first to place the question of domination at the center of their reflections on Kafka's oeuvre. Perhaps because this was not necessarily incompatible with Marxism, or with certain unorthodox readings of Marxist thought. . . . For Benjamin, the critical force of

Kafka comes from the fact that he writes from the point of view of the average citizen—one who knows that he is given over to an impenetrable bureaucratic apparatus whose functioning is controlled by forces that remain unspecified not only in their own protocols, but also, and especially, for those who are subjected to it. Napoleon substituted destiny for politics; in Kafka it's organization that becomes destiny—as we see in the vast hierarchies of *The Trial* and *The Castle*, or in the "inextricable construction projects" as in "The Great Wall of China." Karel Kosik perceives the Kafkaesque world as "a terrifying and absurd labyrinth" in which human beings are "trapped in the web of bureaucratic machinery, of apparatuses, of reified constructions." Finally, Adorno identifies the essential theme of the Prague writer as "blind force endlessly reproducing itself" and ending in "bureaucratic control."[64]

Portrait of Kafka in 1924. Woodcut, 2003. (Sergio Birga.)

Hermann Kafka, the father

Franz Kafka and his favorite sister Ottla

Kafka smiling. No date.

Kafka in 1921

Kafka in Ireland. (Drawing by Guy Girard.)

Chains of official paper (red tape). (Drawing and collage by Guy Girard and Michael Löwy.)

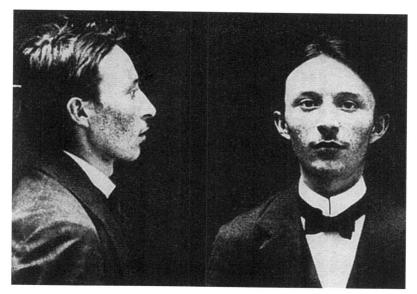

Michal Mares, anarchist poet. (Prague police archives.)

Michal Kacha, one of the principal Prague anarchist leaders

The *Zadruha* (*Commune*) periodical, edited by Michael Kacha

VOLNÉ LISTY.

Entered as second-class matter January 21st 1901 at the Post Office at New York, N. Y. under the Act of Congress of March 3rd, 1879.

ROČ. XVIII. (Vol.)   New York, 23. října (October) 1909.   ČÍS. (NO.) 21.

Francisco FERRER

Petr Kropotkin, anarchist philosopher. A drawing from the Czech
anarchist press.

Francisco Ferrer, Spanish anarchist
educator, shot by firing squad in
1909. A drawing from the Czech
anarchist press.

The Trial (Before the law)
Woodcut, 1963. (Sergio
Birga.)

The Trial. Woodcut, 1963.
(Sergio Birga.)

Drawings by Kafka:
Patriarchal figures

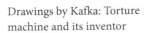

Drawings by Kafka: Torture
machine and its inventor

Drawings by Kafka:
Patriotic parade

CHAPTER 3

KAFKA'S *THE TRIAL*

From the Jew as Pariah to Joseph K. as Universal Victim

In her remarkable essay on the "hidden tradition," published in 1944 in the journal *Jewish Social Studies*, Hannah Arendt presents Franz Kafka—along with Heine, Chaplin, and Bernard Lazare—as one of the most remarkable examples of the pariah-rebel sensibility in the history of modern Jewish culture. According to Arendt, this sensibility, which is based on the experience of exclusion and oppression, questions the very foundations of existing political society.

Arendt goes on to say that the work that expresses this attitude most forcefully is *The Castle*, "the only novel in which Kafka deals with the Jewish question, and the only one in which the hero is clearly Jewish." To be sure, K. has no overt Jewish characteristics, but he finds himself immersed in situations and perplexities "specific to Jewish life."[1] He is a "well-meaning man" who only wishes for his rights to be respected and who aspires only to become an inhabitant of the village like other people. But he sets himself apart from the other villagers, who passively accept being victims of "fate," by wanting to determine his own destiny.[2]

Arendt's reading is interesting, though excessively Judeo-centric: nothing in the novel indicates that the "situations and perplexities"

of K. are specifically Jewish. Quite the opposite—they apply to all
sorts of foreigners and immigrants. Even more problematic is Arendt's attempt to see the political philosophy of the novel in Zionist
terms: Kafka in this interpretation would be a Zionist who would
like to abolish the "abnormal" condition of the Jews, symbolized by
K. At the very least, such an interpretation is perfectly arbitrary and
does not correspond in any way to the gist of the novel, especially
when one bears in mind Kafka's profound ambiguity with relation
to Zionism—an ambiguity summarized in the famous comment of
1918 in his Octavo notebooks: "I . . . have not caught the hem of the
Jewish prayer-mantle—now flying away from us—as the Zionists
have."[3] Admittedly, during the last years of his life, he will evidence
a real interest in certain aspects of the Zionist project: he will even
start learning Hebrew and flirt with the dream of a trip to Palestine.[4] But nothing indicates a real engagement with the movement,
unlike his friend Brod.

A few months after her first essay, Hannah Arendt published another essay on Kafka in the *Partisan Review*, which at that time was
the left-wing organ of anti-Stalinism. Here she revisits her initial positions, but this time she proposes a resolutely universalist reading of
the novel; K. is a foreigner, an immigrant who is fighting for the recognition of his rights.[5] Without a doubt this interpretation is closer to
the spirit and letter of the novel, but her rich and suggestive intuition
about the role of the Jewish pariah-rebel sensibility in Kafka's work
has disappeared. In other words: Arendt's reading of Kafka—which
in many ways is pioneering and startling—lacks a connection between the Jewish and the universal impetus.

Curiously, in the essay in *Jewish Social Studies* that emphasizes the
"Jewishness" of Kafka, *The Trial* is not even mentioned. And yet, in
this novel the "situations and perplexities" are more properly Jewish
than in *The Castle*. Hannah Arendt's silence on the "Jewish" dimension of *The Trial* is all the more surprising in that it is the only novel
of which Kafka published a fragment—the parable *Before the Law*—in
a Jewish (and even Zionist) journal, *Selbstwehr* (*Self-Defense*) edited

by his Prague Jewish friends. In her second article on Kafka in the *Partisan Review*, Arendt talks at length about *The Trial*, but, as with *The Castle*, from a strictly universalist point of view. I will come back to this analysis, which is highly interesting but in which, once again, all reference to Jewish pariahs is absent.

My goal here is simply to take up the thread of her argument where she leaves off. In other words, I want to examine *The Trial* starting from her hypothesis that it expresses the sensibility of the pariah-rebel in Kafka, an approach that I think is profoundly correct. I will try to find a way of connecting this (implicit) "Jewish" dimension of the novel and its authentically universalist content.

Arendt's hypothesis allows one to avoid the conformist readings of *The Trial*. By this I mean two kinds of interpretation of the novel that occupy considerable space in the secondary literature.[6] The first sees the mysterious Tribunal that condemns Joseph K. as a divine institution, to whose decisions one must submit with resignation. The foremost example here is Kafka's great friend and biographer (but mediocre interpreter of his works) Max Brod, who sees the hero/victim of the novel as a sort or modern Job who is hit hard by divine justice. In her second article on Kafka, Arendt subjects this kind of exegesis to a pitiless analysis. Without mentioning anyone specifically, she attacks a person generically described as "a reader from the 20s": the malaise of Kafka's characters comes from "the world's attempt to deify itself, from its presumption to represent itself as divine necessity. Kafka's objective is to destroy this world by exaggerating the contours of its horrible structure . . . but the 1920s reader did not want to listen to reason. His interpretations of Kafka tell us more about him than about Kafka. In his naïve admiration for a world that Kafka had represented as intolerably sinister, the reader revealed his own acceptance of the "world order" and how close the so-called elites and avant-gardes were to this 'world order.'"[7]

Another series of interpreters see Joseph K. as guilty and, therefore, his condemnation as legitimate. Thus Eric Heller—some of whose analyses are worth considering—concludes, after a lengthy discussion of *The Trial*: "There is a certainty that is left untouched by the parable as well as by the whole book: the Law exists and Joseph K. must have terribly offended it, for he is executed in the end with a double-edged . . . butcher's knife that is being thrust into his heart and turned around twice."[8] If applied to the events of the twentieth century, this opinion would mean that if a person, or even millions of people, are executed by the authorities, it's no doubt because they committed a terrible offense against the Law . . . In point of fact, nothing in the novel indicates that Joseph K. "terribly offended" the Law (what Law?) or even less that he deserved the death penalty!

To be sure, other, more attentive readers, while recognizing that nothing in the novel suggests the culpability of the hero, suggest that in the chapters he did not have time to write, Kafka doubtlessly "explained Joseph K.'s transgression or at least the reasons for the trial."[9] One can speculate infinitely about the novel that Kafka would have, or should have written, but in the existing manuscript, one of the most forceful ideas of the text is precisely the absence of any "explanations for the reasons of the trial" and the obstinate refusal of all the concerned bodies—policemen, magistrates, and tribunals—to supply one.

All the attempts of critics to assert the culpability of Joseph K. are inevitably caught short by the first sentence of the novel, which simply affirms: "Someone must have slandered Joseph K., for one morning, without having done anything wrong, he was arrested."[10] It's important to note that this sentence is not at all presented as the subjective opinion of the hero—like those he expresses in many of the novel's passages in which he asserts his innocence—but rather as an "objective" bit of information that is as factual as the next sentence: "Frau Grubach's cook . . . did not appear."[11]

What these different sorts of exegesis have in common is their manner of neutralizing or erasing the novel's formidable critical dimension whose central theme (as Hannah Arendt understood so well) is "the functioning of a nefarious bureaucratic machine in which the innocent hero has become trapped."[12] In describing this functioning, Kafka was no doubt inspired by his work as a lawyer in a bureaucracy, the Workingmen's Accident Insurance Company of the Kingdom of Bohemia. As Max Brod (and many commentators after him) has noted, the description of the opaque and absurd bureaucratic workings in *The Trial* owes much to this daily experience—considered not from the point of view of those at the top but from that of the humble workers with whom Kafka sympathized—the victims of workplace accidents, lost in the administrative labyrinth.

However, the import of the novel lies far beyond this first, rather elemental level; one only needs to think about the ending to realize that what is at stake is much more dramatic. It's not just that bureaucracy is sinister—the real point is that judicial and state institutions are inhumane and murderous.

The prophetic character of the novel is striking—with its visionary imagination it seems to describe the injustice of totalitarian states. Bertolt Brecht was one of the first to notice this, as early as 1937: "At their deepest level, bourgeois democracies contained within themselves fascist dictatorships, and Kafka's grandiose imagination described what would become concentration camps, the absence of any legal guarantees, and the absolute autonomy of the state apparatus."[13] Could one not also apply the same reasoning, mutatis mutandis, to Stalinist Russia? It's Brecht once more (despite being a loyal fellow traveler of the pro-Soviet Communist movement) who, in a conversation with Walter Benjamin about Kafka in 1934 (that is, before the Moscow Trials), said:[14] "Kafka had only one problem, that of organization. What gripped his imagination was his fear of a society of ants: the way in which people become alienated from each other by the forms of their life together. And he foresaw certain forms of this alienation, such as the methods of the Russian Secret Police." And Brecht adds: "You can see from the Gestapo what would become of the Cheka."[15]

These readings offer legitimate praise for the clairvoyance of the Prague writer, who was able to grasp the sinister tendencies that were already lying in wait as potential developments in the "constitutional"

European states at the beginning of the twentieth century. At the same time, it casts little light on Kafka's own motivations and his sources of inspiration. In addition, these a posteriori references to so-called "exception states" risk obfuscating what is one of the most forceful ideas of the novel: the "exception," the crushing of the individual by the state apparatus, in violation of his rights, becomes the rule (to paraphrase a formulation of Walter Benjamin in his "Theses on the Philosophy of History"). In other words: *The Trial* addresses the alienated and oppressive nature of the modern states, including those that describe themselves as "lawful states." This explains why the novel's first pages clearly indicate that "after all, K. has rights, the country was at peace, the laws have not been suspended—who then, had the audacity to descend on him in the privacy of his own home?"[16] Like his Prague anarchist friends, Kafka seems to consider any form of the existing state as an authoritarian hierarchy based on illusion and lies.

One shouldn't look into future events, but rather into contemporary historical events for *The Trial*'s source of inspiration.[17] Among these events, the great anti-Semitic trials of his time constituted a flagrant example of state injustice. The most famous were the trials of Tisza (Hungary, 1882), Dreyfus (France, 1894–1899), Hilsner (Czechoslovakia, 1899–1900), and Beiliss (Russia, 1912–1913). Despite the differences between the types of state—absolutist, constitutional monarchy, republic—the judicial system condemned, sometimes to death, innocent victims whose only crime was that they were Jewish.

The Tisza affair—a trial in 1882–1883 for ritual murder against fifteen members of a Jewish community in the north of Hungary—could not have touched Kafka directly, because he was born in 1883. However, in a letter to Felice Bauer dated October 28, 1916, one finds a moving reference to the play by the Jewish-German writer Arnold Zweig, *Ritualmord in Ungarn* (*Ritual Murder in Hungary*, written in Berlin in 1914), which treats this subject: "The other day I read 'Ritual Murder in Hungary,' a tragedy by Zweig; its supernatural scenes are as contrived and feeble as I would have expected from what I know of

Zweig's work. The earthly scenes on the other hand are intensely alive, taken no doubt largely from the excellent record of the case. Nevertheless one cannot quite distinguish between the two worlds; he has identified himself with the case and is now under its spell. I no longer see him the way I used to. At one point I had to stop reading, sit down on the sofa, and weep. It's years since I wept."[18]

On the other hand, we don't know what he thought of the Dreyfus trial, which is rarely mentioned in his writings and then only in passing, as in a letter to Max Brod from 1922,[19] even if we can be more or less sure that, like any European (and Jewish) citizen of his generation, he was familiar with the principal episodes of this traumatic event.

As for the Hilsner trial, despite his youth (sixteen years of age), Kafka did not fail to grasp its disquieting scope. The young Jew Leopold Hilsner, who had been condemned to death for "ritual murder" despite an absence of proof, was saved only thanks to the campaign of Tomas Masaryk, a leading political democrat (the future president of the Czechoslovak Republic). During a retrial, his sentence was commuted to life imprisonment. In a conversation reported by Gustav Janouch, Kafka mentioned this trial as the starting point, in the course of discussions with his high school classmate Hugo Bergmann, for his awareness of the Jewish condition. He comments that Hilsner was treated as "a despised individual, considered by the surrounding world a foreigner that is barely tolerated,"[20] in other words a *pariah*.

Of course, one must treat Janouch's reports with caution, but in a letter to Milena dated June 20, 1920, we have a direct reference to the Hilsner affair, as a paradigmatic example of the irrationality of anti-Semitic prejudice: "I can't imagine how people . . . could have conceived of the idea of ritual murder." In a sort of fantastical spectacle, "Hilsner is seen as committing his crime step by step." Other letters to Milena contain additional references to anti-Semitism.[21]

Finally, it's possible that the trial of the Jewish tailor Mendel Beiliss (accused of "ritual murder" in Kiev in 1913) disturbed him even more.

The journal *Selbstwehr* (to which he subscribed) put its resources into covering the affair, which demonstrated in a remarkable fashion the way that Jews were seen as "pariahs" in the Russian empire. They lacked rights, were socially excluded, and were persecuted by the state. We know that among the papers that Kafka burned shortly before his death was a tale about Mendel Beiliss.[22]

That the anti-Semitic trials, particularly this last one, were sources for *The Trial* is just a hypothesis. But it is rendered more plausible by the circumstance that after 1911 and his encounter with the Yiddish theater and his friendship with the actor Itzhak Löwy, Kafka developed a growing interest in Judaism—evidenced, among other things, by his sending his writings to Jewish publications such as *Selbstwehr* (the journal of Prague Zionists) and *Der Jude* (the journal headed by Martin Buber). At the same time, he reacted to these trials not only as a Jew, but also as a universal spirit, *discovering in the Jewish experience the quintessential human experience in the modern era.* In *The Trial* Joseph K. has no specific nationality or religion: the very choice of a simple initial in place of a name reinforces his identity as universal man: he is the representation par excellence of the victims of the legal machinery of the state.[23]

In a recent commentary on Hannah Arendt's concept of the pariah, Eleni Varikas underlines its importance for criticism and the paradigmatic status embodied by the marginalized experience of pariahs: "As the product and symptom of a political understanding in which, because of the dominance of Western traditions, human diversity is dealt with only marginally (Hannah Arendt),"[24] the pariah illuminates not only dysfunction and failure, but also the nature and limits of historical, that is to say state, democracy.[25] For instance the "lawful state" (*Rechtsstaat*) comes in the early morning to arrest innocent civilians, as in the first paragraph of Kafka's *The Trial*.

In his universalist reinterpretation of the anti-Semitic trials, Kafka's sympathy for antiauthoritarian ideas no doubt played a large part. The issue of the "injustice of the state" plays a large role in anarchist culture, which annually commemorates on May 1 the "Chicago martyrs," the falsely accused anarchist union leaders executed in 1886. In 1909 another affair had aroused the indignation of anarchist and progressive circles all over the world: the sentencing and execution of Francisco Ferrer, the eminent libertarian socialist educator and founder of the Modern School, falsely accused of having inspired an anarchist-unionist uprising in Barcelona. According to Michael Mares, Kafka participated in a protest demonstration in Prague against the Spanish monarchy's execution of Ferrer.

Once again, the novels of Kafka are far from being the vehicles of any political or doctrinal "message"; but they do express a certain antiauthoritarian state of mind and a critical and ironic distance from the hierarchies of bureaucratic and judicial power. A striking example of this irony is to be found in the fragment "The Assistant Public Prosecutor" (in the posthumous notebooks), where Kafka humorously portrays the servile, stultified, and authoritarian reasoning of a prosecutor confronted with a man accused of lèse-majesté: "If everyone were calmly and trustfully loyal to the King and the Government, it would be possible to remove all difficulties . . . the more trustful one was, the better it was, and the more trustful one was, the more deeply one must bow in a natural expression of one's attitude, without sycophancy."[26]

How is this judicial hierarchy presented in *The Trial*? Essentially, it's from the subjective point of view of the victim Joseph K., with the addition of some information provided by people who claim to be close to the Tribunal (the painter, the lawyer). The confusing explanations that they give about the functioning of the system express the author's ironic stance toward the perverse logic of the judicial bureaucracy.

Joseph K. is arrested one morning, apparently the victim of a slur. One could interpret this statement as an indirect reference to the anti-Semitic trials, but the problem of the slur is not pursued in the novel. Everyone refuses to give him any explanation for the arrest—which does not take the form of incarceration, but rather of a menace suspended above his head, since he is allowed to continue his regular occupations. He is judged by a Tribunal that denies him any access to his judges, and which barely "tolerates" him rather than taking his defense into account. This Tribunal, whose hierarchy extends to infinity (*unendlich*), claims infallibility and is inaccessible to the accused: its workings are secret and the act of accusation itself is not communicated to the interested party (nor to the lawyers or, naturally, the general public). Therefore the accused is incapable of defending himself, since he doesn't know what he has been accused of. After a completely obscure procedure, the Tribunal sends a couple of executioners to kill the unfortunate Joseph K. The true character of this justice is ironically portrayed by an allegory when the painter Titorelli represents the goddess of Justice as a goddess of Victory, or rather, once the contours of the painting emerge, as a goddess of the Hunt.[27]

The law is practically absent in this "trial." It is something unknown, unknowable, nonexistent. Its absence is compensated by the presence, or rather omnipresence, of a formidable legal organization that has the power of life and death over individuals. In one of the novel's most intense moments, Joseph K. indignantly denounces it, as "an organization which not only employs venal guards, foolish supervisors, and examining magistrates who are at best unassuming, but which, beyond that, doubtless maintains a bench of judges of high, indeed the highest standing, with their inevitable numerous entourage of ushers, clerks, police officers, and other assistants, perhaps even, I do not hesitate to use the word, executioners. And the point of this large organization, gentlemen? It consists in arresting innocent persons and instituting pointless and mostly, as in my case, fruitless proceedings against them."[28] Considering the dramatic conclusion of the novel, this reference to executioners is significant: it demonstrates the hero's clairvoyance, despite his dangerous underestimation of the Tribunal. In any case, during his conversation with Titorelli, Joseph K. summarizes his poor opinion of the judicial institution: "The whole court could be replaced by a single executioner."[29] Joseph K. conducts a solitary battle against the Tribunal—this is perhaps one of the reasons for his defeat—but he is aware that he is not the only victim of this "justice," which proceeds in the same way against a multitude of people. In one of his visits to the Tribunal, he encounters other defendants—humiliated and frightened, and standing around "like beggars in the street."[30]

Is this description of the functioning of the judicial institutions "realistic?" Perhaps it's the wrong question. In the passage cited above, Hannah Arendt talks about Kafka's "exaggerations"; but one wonders whether the realities of the twentieth century have not greatly surpassed the blackest images of the novel. "Realist" or not, Kafka succeeded in depicting, like no one before him (and probably no one since), the functioning of the judicial machine *from the point of view of its victims*. He manages this without pathos, with rigor and sobriety, in a style characterized by an austerity and simplicity that makes it all the more impressive. The universality of the novel and its strong element of subjectivity—its focus on those who fall under the wheels of the triumphant chariot of "justice"—made *The Trial* one of the works that had the strongest appeal to the twentieth-century imagination.

How can one resist the murderous churning of state justice? Kafka's Zionist friends believed that the Jewish pariahs had to organize themselves in self-defense (*Selbstwehr*), as a first step toward restoring their dignity. For his Prague anarchist friends, the only defense was direct action by the oppressed against the power of the oppressor. Kafka probably sympathized with these attitudes, but what he shows in *The Trial* is less optimistic and more "realistic"—namely the defeat and resignation of the victim. Joseph K.'s first reaction is resistance and (individual) rebellion: he denounces, protests, and expresses with sarcasm and irony his disdain for the institution that is supposed to render its judgment on him. He also tends to underestimate the danger. Those whom he asks for help advise submission. Leni, the servant of the lawyer, tells him, "No one can resist this court, you just have to confess. Confess at the first opportunity."[31] As for the lawyer himself, his advice to K. is simply to "accept things as they were," and "not to attract attention, to stay calm, however much it went against the grain."[32] Joseph K. refuses this "friendly" advice; he has nothing but contempt for servile characters, whom he compares to dogs.

In many of Kafka's novels, the dog appears as the allegorical figure of voluntary servitude, of the behavior of those who lie down at the feet of those higher than they in the hierarchy and blindly obey the voice of their masters. In *The Trial*, the lawyer Huld "demeans himself just like a dog before the Tribunal." At a lower level in the hierarchy, the corn merchant Block falls to his knees before Huld and behaves in an abjectly servile manner: "Such a person was no longer a client, he was the lawyer's dog. If the lawyer had ordered him to crawl under the bed, as if going into a kennel, and bark, he would have done so with pleasure."[33] Then, in the last chapter of the novel, Joseph K.'s behavior changes radically. After a brief show of resistance—"I'm not going any farther"—he decides, after seeing the mysterious and distant apparition of his neighbor, Fräulein Bürstner, that resistance is futile, and he obliges (*Entgegenkommen*) his executioners in perfect agreement (*vollem Einverständnis*) with their intentions.[34] He is not only resigned to his fate, but seems to want to actively cooperate with his punishment. It's only from a lack of strength that he fails to accomplish what he thinks of as his "duty": to take the weapon in his own hands and kill himself. Still, at the moment that the executioners plunge the knife into his heart he has time to pronounce, before dying, "Like a dog!" And the last sentence of the novel is a commentary: "It seemed as if his shame would live on after him."[35] What shame? Without a doubt, that of dying submissively, "like a dog," in a state of voluntary servitude (in the sense that Étienne de la Boétie uses the term).[36] ⌐

How can one explain Joseph K.'s change of attitude? It's useless to speculate about unwritten chapters. The novel's ending offers few explanations. There is only the strange interior monologue of the character that hardly sheds light on the matter: "Am I now going to show that I have not learnt anything from a trial that lasted almost a year? Am I going to depart as a slow-witted person?"[37] In her *Partisan Re-*

view article, Hannah Arendt proposes an explanation based on Joseph K.'s internalized feeling of guilt: "In *The Trial*, submission is not obtained by force, but rather by the growing sense of guilt that K. begins to feel because of the empty and false accusation. . . . The functioning of the nefarious bureaucratic machine that entraps the innocent hero is accompanied by an internal development that comes from a feeling of culpability. . . . The internal development of the hero and the functioning of the machine finally meet in the last scene, at the execution, where the unresisting and uncomplaining K. allows himself to be taken and killed."[38]

Her hypothesis is interesting and plausible. The problem is that nothing in this remarkable final chapter of *The Trial*—about six or seven pages long, and composed from the very beginning of Kafka's writing the novel—indicates that Joseph K. considered himself to be guilty. The question of culpability is never invoked in these dense and enigmatic pages. One knows only that after adjusting his pace to the rhythm of that of the two executioners, K. considers it his "duty" to sacrifice himself. Should one see this scene as a cryptic reference to the voluntary servitude of the soldiers who, in August 1914, marched in step, enthusiastically and joyfully, to the front, impatient to sacrifice their lives for their country? Let us recall that Franz Kafka—who in 1909–1912 had participated in the public meetings of the antimilitarist club Vilem Körber—had started to write *The Trial* in August 1914, just a few days after the outbreak of the First World War. It's at this moment also—on August 6, 1914—that he notes in his *Diaries*: "Patriotic parade . . . I stand there with my evil eye. These parades are one of the most disgusting accompaniments of the war."[39]

In any event, the conclusion of the novel is at the same time "pessimistic" and resolutely nonconformist. It expresses Kafka's sentiments as a rebel-pariah, who reveals in these pages at the same time compassion for the victim and a critique of his voluntary submission. One can read them as a call to resistance.[40]

CHAPTER 4

THE RELIGION OF LIBERTY AND THE PARABLE *BEFORE THE LAW* (1915)

Was Kafka religious? In a letter to Grete Bloch dated June 11, 1914, he describes himself as an asocial person, excluded from the community because of his "non-Zionist, non-practicing Judaism (I admire Zionism and am nauseated by it)."[1] If one examines his notes and aphorisms, it seems that he constantly hesitates between faith and doubt. Sometimes he asserts his confidence in "something indestructible" in mankind, one of whose possibilities for expression is "faith in a personal God"; yet in the very next paragraph, he drily observes: "The heavens are silent, echoing back only to the mute" (*Der Himmel ist stumm, nur dem Stummen Widerhall*).[2] The hypothesis that we would like to examine here is the following: Franz Kafka's structure of feeling is neither directly religious nor purely secular, but is situated in a sort of twilight, of "no mans land," of threshold between these opposite poles. In his already canonical essay *A Secular Age*, Charles Taylor has an interesting insight: the Romantic protests against disenchantment can take both religious and secular forms. However, "in the face of the opposition between orthodoxy and unbelief, many, and among them the best and the most sensitive minds, were . . . looking for a third way."[3] I think Franz Kafka is one of those "best and most sensitive minds . . ."

This ambivalent "third way," this subtle imbrication of hope and despair, finds expression sometimes in one and the same passage, as in this enigmatic parable about light: "Seen with the terrestrial sullied eye, we are in the situation of travellers in a train that has met with an accident in a tunnel, and this at a place where the light of the beginning can no longer be seen, and the light of the end is so very small a glimmer that the gaze must continually search for it and is always losing it again, and furthermore, both the beginning and the end are not even certainties."[4]

Despite this, it is undeniable that a strange atmosphere of religiosity impregnates the great unfinished novels of Kafka. Is it related to Jewish messianism? How to characterize this spirituality—mysterious, diffuse, ambivalent? Leaving to one side the controversial question of its sources—Kierkegaard, the Gnostics, the kabbalah, the Bible, or Hasidism—what is the structure and significance of this religious vision? Is it a positive messianism, full of hope and faith, as Max Brod seems to think? Despite his attempt to try at any price to construct a "positive" image of his friend, Brod himself is forced to admit that the great novels and sketches are dominated by negativism: he tries nevertheless to cover it up by attributing it to Kafka's "inventive genius" and his "supremely terrifying imagination."[5]

The messianic dimension of Kafka's writing is treated in the correspondence between Gershom Scholem and Walter Benjamin in 1934–1935. Commenting on these exchanges, Scholem will later write in an essay on his friend: "In Kafka's world, Benjamin finds the negative inversion (*negativen Umschlag*) of Jewish categories. No more positive doctrine. There only subsists . . . a kind of utopian promise that one can't yet put into words. . . . Benjamin knew that one finds in Kafka the *theologia negativa* of a Judaism that has lost the positive sense of Revelation without losing any of its intensity."[6]

It seems to me that the concept of negative theology is the only one, in fact, that can adequately address the problem of the very particular kind of religious problematic present in the works of

Kafka. This means, for Scholem, a theology of the *absence of* God, and not, as in the traditional conception—for instance, in Maimonides—a theology that denies the possibility of knowing God's positive attributes.

Messianic redemption—and also, as we have seen, libertarian socialist utopianism—exists in Kafka only insofar as it is hollowed out, traced in filigree around the black contours of the present world. In other words, the works of Kafka describe a world given over to the absurd, to authoritarian injustice, and to untruth, a world without liberty where messianic redemption manifests itself only negatively by its radical absence. As Adorno so tellingly writes, in Kafka "the wounds with which society brands (*einbrennt*) the individual are seen by the latter as ciphers of the social untruth, as the negative of truth."[7] Not only is there no positive message—but the messianic promise of the future lies only with the implicit and perhaps religious way of considering (and rejecting) the contemporary world as infernal. The "theology" of Kafka—if one can use the term—is therefore negative in a precise sense: its object is the nonpresence of God in the world and the nonredemption of humankind. This reversal, this negative overturning (*Gegenstück*), is apparent not only in the novels but also in the paradoxes that inform his aphorisms.

In the political sphere, a sort of *utopia negativa* corresponds to Kafka's *theologia negativa* or negative messianism. There is a remarkable structural analogy between the two: in both cases, the positive reversal of the world thus established (libertarian utopia or messianic redemption) is radically absent; and it is precisely this absence that defines human life as fallen, or void of meaning. The absence of redemption, the religious indicator of an era that is damned, corresponds to the absence of liberty in the suffocating world of bureaucratic arbitrariness. The underlying elective affinity between these two "negative" configurations ends here in a close convergence that fashions the significative structure of the novels: the crushing of the individual ("Like a dog!"),[8] the supreme denial of liberty—these are precisely the indices of the nonredemption of the world; on the other hand, the limitless (religious) liberty of the individual would announce the arrival of the Messiah.

The elective affinity between negative theology and negative utopia probably constitutes one of the essential components of the enigmatic and singular spiritual quality of Kafka's writings.[9]

Kafka's burning aspiration for liberty is not an ideology but, as we saw, an existential attitude. Few texts condense this attitude as intensely as the parable *Before the Law* (*Vor dem Gesetz*). This is one of the most famous of Kafka's texts and one of the few to have been published during his lifetime. This passage of *The Trial* was also one of his favorites, one that he liked to read to his friends and to his fiancée Felice.[10] In his *Diaries* he calls it a "fable" and, in the novel, simply a "story." But the term *parable* (*Gleichnis*) that he often uses to designate these short and highly paradoxical texts, disseminated throughout his notebooks and his *Diaries* like sparkling gems, is perhaps the most appropriate.

It's no accident that this text—one of the two chapters of *The Trial* published during Kafka's lifetime—was sent by its author to the periodical *Selbstwehr* (*Self-Defense*) of the Bar Kochba Circle in Prague, which published it in 1915: even if he did not necessarily share the Zionist doctrine of this publication, Kafka was not indifferent to its ideal of self-emancipation.

This polysemic and enigmatic text seems to concentrate, in a few paragraphs, the essence of Kafka's spirituality: it throws a powerful light not only on *The Trial* itself, but on the whole of the Prague author's work. It's a paradoxical text, at the same time tender and cruel, simple and terribly complex, transparent and opaque, luminous and dark. It represents Kafka's art in full force, and it is not surprising that it has continued to haunt readers and critics for more than a century.

The outlines of this parable, which is told to Joseph K. by a priest during his visit to the cathedral, are well known: a man from the country comes to ask for access to the law; but the doorkeeper (*To-*

rhüter) of the Law explains to him that he is unable to authorize him to enter. He himself is only the first of the doorkeepers, whereas the others, on the inside, are much more powerful. The man waits in vain for permission to enter. Seated on a wooden stool, he waits for many long years and eventually grows old there. As he lies dying, he asks a final question: "So how is it that in all these years no one apart from me has asked to be let in?" The doorkeeper shouts into his ear: "No one else could be granted entry here, because this entrance was intended for you alone. I shall now go and shut it."[11]

By its very nature as a "canonical" and quasi-biblical document, the fable has given rise to interpretations, attempts at deciphering, explanations, and counterexplanations, a delirium of interpretation, *disputationes*, and controversies. Is the Law of the parable a divine— as the Jewish Torah—or a human one ? What was the man's mistake ? Was he a victim of the doorkeeper? Kafka himself engages heartily in this exercise; the parable is followed by a long theological and hermeneutic debate between Joseph K. and the priest about the meaning of the narrative—a debate that remains inconclusive and leaves all the questions in suspension. Kafka seems to share with other secular Jews a Talmudic obsession with interpretation and an insistence that everything has a meaning[12]—even if the meaning remains open and undecided.

While Joseph K. can't refrain from believing that the man was deceived by the doorkeeper, the priest responds with the classic argument of clerics: to doubt the dignity of the doorkeeper would be to "doubt the law." The authority of the doorkeeper is greatly superior to the truth: "You don't have to think that everything is true, it's enough to believe that it is necessary." This apologetic reasoning is spontaneously rejected by Joseph K., who defines it, in an extraordinarily powerful formulation, as the sign of a universally fallen world: "A depressing opinion. . . . It means that the world order is founded on untruth" (*die Lüge wird zur Weltordnung gemacht*).[13]

What can this parable possibly mean? Despairing of making sense of it, some readers admit their perplexity. No one has expressed this despair with more talent and grace than Jacques Derrida, in a brilliant lecture in 1982 titled "Prejudices." After calling in vain upon Kant, Freud, and Heidegger, the philosopher admits: "I have proposed tentative glosses, multiplied interpretations, asked questions and turned them around, abandoned attempts at deciphering" in order to, at the end, "leave enigmas intact." Nevertheless, two of the approaches he suggests seem very interesting. Here is the first: "By his very situation, the man from the country does not know the law, which is always the law of the city, the law of towns and buildings, protected edifices, iron gates and limits, spaces closed off by doors."[14] Barriers and iron gates—*cancelli* in Latin, which gave rise to the German *Kanzlei*—are devoid of religious signification and demystified as obstacles erected by humans.

The second approach also concerns the behavior of the man from the country: "The man is in possession of a natural or physical freedom to enter into places, including into the law. Therefore, as one . . . must admit, he has to forbid himself from entering." The Law "allows the man to 'freely' determine himself, despite the fact that this freedom is annulled by his self-imposed interdiction to enter the Law." It seems to me that Derrida here touches upon what is really at stake in this fable, but he soon turns away to conclude (but is it really a conclusion?) with a statement about the "illegibility of the text, if we mean by that our inability to arrive at its true meaning, at the perhaps inconsistent content that it jealously keeps in reserve." In other words: "We are *before* this text that, saying nothing with clarity, and presenting no identifiable content beyond its narrative except for an interminable delay until death, nevertheless remains rigorously intangible. By intangible I mean inaccessible to contact, impregnable, and, in the end, elusive and incomprehensible."[15]

Most exegetes refuse to be satisfied with this kind of *protocol of opacity* and try, in spite of everything, with more or less success, to find the parable's substratum of truth. Some of these readings seem to me misunderstandings—they simply pass to the side of what is essential. This is notably the case with Max Brod, who compares the parable to the book of Job, both literally and in spirit: "God's will appears to our eyes illogical or rather grotesquely opposed to our human logic. . . . In the Book of Job, God acts similarly in ways that appear absurd and unjust to man. But this is just how they appear to humans, and the final conclusion, in the case of Job as for Kafka, is that human measures are not those of the world of the Absolute."[16] The trouble with this passably naive interpretation—which, according to Brod, applies not only to the parable but also to the great novels, *The Trial* and *The Castle*—is that nothing in Kafka's writings suggest this "ultimate conclusion."

One can apply the same skepticism to the reading by Hartmut Binder, who, after two hundred pages of erudite exegesis, concludes that the parable is a sort of allegory that embodies the impasse, or double bind, in certain human relations (*Beziehungsfallen*), such as those of Kafka with his parents or with his fiancée Felice.[17] Finally, Giuliano Baioni, whose book is sometimes full of interesting observations, takes a wrong turn when he writes that the function of the parable in the novel is "eminently aesthetic": it represents "the perfection of formal attributes" or even "the necessity of form against the arbitrariness of chaos."[18] What is lost in this kind of interpretation is the *critical* dimension, the profoundly *subversive* aspect of the text in both the political and religious sense.

One cannot understand this text without situating it within a larger context: Kafka's spirituality, his ethical and social convictions, and, in particular, his libertarian-inspired antiauthoritarianism. How could this antiauthoritarianism—an existential attitude, *Sitz im Leben*, more than a political choice—not translate itself also onto the terrain of religion? It takes the form of the refusal of any power that claims to represent divinity and to impose dogmas, doctrines, and prohibitions in its name. It's not so much divine authority that is questioned—if its existence is even acknowledged—but rather the authority of religious institutions, clerics, and other doorkeepers of the Law. The religion of Kafka, to the extent that one can use this expression, would be a sort of *religion of liberty* (the term comes from his friend Felix Weltsch) in the strongest and most absolute sense of the term—one inspired by heterodox Judaism.

The sources of this spirituality are not to be found in faraway and mysterious esoteric doctrines—like the Gnostics or the kabbalah often mentioned by researchers—but rather in the writings of some of his closest Jewish friends in Prague: Hugo Bergmann and Felix Weltsch. One should apply to these sources the method suggested by Scott Spector : they should not be considered as "secret referents to be uncovered" but as "found objects used for the construction of entirely new, open and evocative literary figures."[19]

Kafka's childhood friend and high-school classmate Hugo Bergmann published, in the 1913 Prague anthology *Vom Judentum* (which Kafka knew, since it appears in his library), an essay titled "The Sanctification of the Name" (*Kiddush Hashem*). According to Bergmann, what distinguishes human beings from the world of objects in Judaism is precisely *liberty*, the freedom of deciding, the capacity to free oneself from the network of conditioning, to refuse limitations. In Jewish understanding, the human being is at the same time creature and creator. Humans are *creatures* when they, like things, are moved by exterior forces; but *creators* when, liberating themselves from the chain of external necessities, they freely rise to ethical action. "As a moral being, the human being is his own creator (*Selbstschöpfer*), as the Talmud explicitly states (Sanhédrin 99b). And here—in the language of the Zohar (I, 9b, 10a)—the task of the human being is expressed: to no longer be a cistern, simple recipient of water from the outside, but to become a spring that generates its own water."[20]

The attitude of Kafka toward Hugo Bergmann is not without ambiguity, in a mixture of friendship, respect, and critical distance. An interesting note in the *Diaries* dated December 17, 1913, mentions a lecture by his friend titled "Moses and the Present." This probably refers to a text that was later published with a slightly different title, "Pessah and the Human Beings of Our Era." In it Bergmann pays homage to Moses, who brought to Jews "the Gospel of liberty and of action," and contrasts him with contemporary Jews, "slaves of conditioning, of compromises, of untruth." The conclusion comes in the form of a question: "Will we be able to free ourselves from the chains of our times?"[21] At first Kafka praises his friend, making much of the "pure impression" that his words afford him. But this is only to immediately dissociate himself from them: "In any case, I have nothing to do with this." Is he referring to the Zionism that permeates the whole lecture, or to the criticism of contemporary Jews? It's hard to decide. As for the next sentence, it seems to suggest a favorable attitude once more: "The true and terrible paths between freedom and slavery cross each other with no guide to the way ahead and accompanied by an immediate erasure of the paths already traversed."[22] It seems to me that this commentary is less a summary of Bergmann's lecture than Kafka's own thought progression on the basis of it. In any case, it undeniably signals that "religion of liberty" which, in a way, is shared by both.[23]

As for Felix Weltsch, who had been one of Kafka's closest friends since 1912, one finds, in his 1920 book *Gnade und Freiheit* (*Mercy and Liberty*) a celebration of Judaism as the "religion of liberty," allowing for the metaphysical and even "magical" possibility of the intervention of free will in the world. According to Felix Weltsch, in the Hebraic tradition one also finds a "religion of mercy"; but it's the "religion of liberty" that predominates in the kabbalah as in Hasidism, and that is developed further in German thinking (Schelling, Fichte) as well as in contemporary Judaism (Buber). While the belief in mercy leads to quietism, belief in liberty leads to activism and to an ethic of action in liberty that constitutes its own value, independently of its success or failure. In a letter to his friend, Kafka had expressed his great interest in this book and, in particular, in its final chapter titled "Creative Freedom as Religious Principle" (*Schöpferische Freiheit als religiöses Prinzip*).[24] His sympathy for Felix Weltsch's voluntarism also transpires from certain passages of the *Diaries*, as for instance in December 16, 1913, where he pays homage to his friend's self-confidence by summarizing his philosophy as "One must want the impossible."[25]

It goes without saying that Kafka was not necessarily in agreement with all of his friends' ideas and that one would never explain his own spirituality by citing any sort of "influence." Despite this, it is undeniable that there exists a sort of affinity or "family resemblance" between the works of Huge Bergmann and Felix Weltsch, on the one hand, and, on the other, certain texts of Kafka with a religious emphasis. Of course, Kafka was neither a theologian nor a philosopher, as a writer he engaged in an aesthetic activity which did not deal with concepts and doctrines, but with imaginary creations.

The case of Max Brod is different, because he is much more hesitant and eclectic. Adhering at first to a strict Schopenhauerian determinism, he ended up embracing the religion of liberty through the combined influence of Bergmann and Weltsch. The most successful literary expression of this is his 1915 novel *Tycho Brahes Weg zu Gott* (*Tycho Brahe's Way to God*), an autobiographical work that celebrates the human being's capacity for free choice. The author dedicated this work to Kafka. Nevertheless, a few years later, after a personal crisis, Max Brod distanced himself from this activist conception of religion (which is founded on the idea that God himself depends on human action) in order to become, in the 1920 *Heidentum, Christentum, Judentum* (*Paganism, Christianity, Judaism*), the apostle of a theology of divine mercy (*Gnade*) and human impotence. As much as Kafka admired his friend's first work, he had many reservations about the second. In a letter to Max Brod on August 7, 1920, he criticizes what seems to him an unjust representation of paganism: the religious universe of the Greeks "was less profound than Jewish Law, but perhaps more democratic (there were no leaders or founders of religions), perhaps freer (it held, but I don't know how)."[26] What seems important to me in this passage is less the provocative praise of paganism than the idealized image of a free and "democratic" religion without leaders or authorities.

Kafka's relation to literature is also impregnated with this "gospel of liberty." The opposition between his professional and family life and literary creation—this permanent rift that returns like a plaintive note all through his *Diaries*—is often presented as an antagonism between enslavement and liberty: "Yet if I wish to transcend the initial pangs of writing (as well as the inhibiting effect of my way of life) and rise up into the freedom that perhaps awaits me, I know that I must not yield."[27]

Kafka's "religion of liberty" and his critique of religious authority find their purest expression in the troubling parable *Before the Law*. Among the many schools of interpretation that this mysterious and fascinating text has elicited for more than a century, it seems to me that the most pertinent is the one that regards the doorkeeper as the representative, not of divine justice—before which the man from the country, like Job, would find himself helpless—but rather as the representative of that world order based on untruth that Joseph K. talks about. The first to interpret the parable in this way is none other than Felix Weltsch, who, true to his philosophy of liberty, states, in an article published in 1927, that the man from the country fails because he lacked the will to take the road to the Law by going through the door *without permission*.[28]

In other words, the man from the country has *let himself be intimidated*: he is not kept from entering by force, but by fear, lack of self-confidence, false obedience to authority, and submissive passivity.[29] If he is lost, it's because "he doesn't dare place his own personal law above the collective taboos whose tyranny is personified in the doorkeeper."[30] In some ways, the doorkeeper is a superpowerful paternal image, who prevents his son from entering into his own independent life. The underlying reason why the man has not traversed the barrier to enter the Law and life is fear, hesitation, lack of determination. The timidity and angst of he who begs the right to enter is precisely what allows the doorkeeper to block his path.[31]

As for religious authority, the argument of the priest (or rather the prison chaplain) whose specious theological discourse tries to justify the position of the doorkeeper as "not true but necessary" represents, according to Hannah Arendt, "the bureaucrats' secret theology and intimate belief in necessity in and for itself—since bureaucrats in the final analysis are functionaries of necessity." The "necessity" claimed by the priest is not that of the Law, but that of the corrupt and fallen laws of the world that prevent access to truth.[32] It seems to me that this interpretation is the only one that is coherent with the antiauthoritarian sensibility that, as it were, illuminates from the inside the entire oeuvre of Kafka. At the same time it should be emphasized that the parable has no "normative" intention: the writer is not telling the reader "what should be done." He is only giving a literary—that is, aesthetic—expression to a certain *Stimmung*, a highly vulnerable and subjective structure of feeling.

In style and spirit *Before the Law* has often been compared to Talmudic texts, to midrashim (exegeses), Haggadoth (tales), or Hasidic stories. Several interpreters have insisted on its resemblance with one of the Hasidic fables of Nachman of Bratzlav, collected by Martin Buber in the 1906 *Die Geschichten des Rabbi Nachman* (*The Tales of Rabbi Nachman*), titled "The Rabbi and His Only Son." It's the tale of a rabbi whose remarkably talented son ardently desires to visit a zaddik (one of the "just," a Hasidic charismatic leader) who lives at a distance of several days of travel from their village. The father, who is a sworn enemy of Hasidism, is opposed to the trip and tries to prevent his son from leaving by all sorts of arguments and obstacles. Finally, in despair over the impossibility of accomplishing his desire, the son dies, whereupon it's the father, in sadness and full of guilt, who makes the trip to the zaddik.[33] Of course one can assume that Kafka, like most cultured German Jews of his generation, had read Buber's book, but I am unable to find even the least meaningful similarity between this tale and the parable *Before the Law*, other than a very general formal aspect: obstacles prevent an individual from attaining his goal until he dies.[34]

On the other hand one can't avoid being struck by a surprising analogy (recently noted by a German researcher) between the Kafka fable and *Pesikta Rabbati*, a narrative from the midrash about the ascension of Moses to heaven during his stay on Mount Sinai. Arriving at the gates of heaven, Moses sees his way blocked by a guardian angel, Kemuel, who prohibits him from acceding to the residence of the Most High. The prophet unhesitatingly knocks him down and continues on his way in the heavens. Soon he is confronted by the second and the third guardian angels, each of whom is much more powerful than the first. The second is six hundred times larger than the first, and Moses can't even approach the third, because he would be consumed in his fire. This is an almost literal version of the doorkeeper's statement in Kafka's text: "The third doorkeeper is so powerful that even I cannot bear to look at him." In the midrash, Moses is finally admitted to the presence of the Most High, who helps him to pass by the dangerous guardian angels.[35] In comparing the two narratives, what is interesting is at the same time the similarity (even though there is no proof that Kafka was familiar with this midrash) and the difference: unlike the man from the country, the Hebrew prophet did not let himself be discouraged by the guardian of the gate, and, thanks to his determined action, he opened his way to the Law.

Kafka never concealed his admiration for people who have the courage to follow their chosen path despite the prohibitions of convention. In a November 1920 letter to E. Mitze, there is a passage that seems like a commentary about the 1915 fable: the writer recommends to his female friend *Memorien einer Sozialistin* (*Memoirs of a Socialist Woman*) by Lily Braun, whom he describes as an admirable woman who "suffered greatly from the morality of her class (such morality is false in any case; it's only beyond it that the darkness of conscience begins), but she forged her path, fighting like a militant angel."[36] While the man from the country, intimidated by the menace of the terrible guardian angels of the Law, acquiesced to the mendacious order of the world, the socialist woman refused the mendacious morality of her class (the bourgeoisie) and dared to go forward, "fighting like a militant angel."

It's in 1914–1915, while he was writing *The Trial* (and therefore the parable *Before the Law*) that Kafka comes across the book of Lily Braun; he sends a copy to his fiancée Felice Bauer in April 1915 and later sends copies to several friends: "By the way I recently gave Max

[Brod] a copy of the *Memoirs*, and I am about to give one to Ottla; I'm giving them away right and left. They are more appropriate for this day and age and more to the point than anything else I know, as well as being the liveliest encouragement."[37] Why this enthusiasm? In many ways the ideas of this socialist woman are similar to the Prague writer's "religion of liberty": "I have built the church of my religion slowly, laboriously laying one stone upon another. I was invaded by a feeling of happiness when I saw that my work was complete, and I made the firm decision not to accept any profession of faith other than my own."[38]

Following the precepts of Shelley ("Do not be afraid! Wage war against domination and lies!") and of Nietzsche ("Obey thyself!"), Lily Braun condemns "submission, humiliation, abandoning oneself to fate and disobeying oneself in order to obey one's superiors." Finally, she makes the distinction between the "will to action" of the free person and the "resignation of powerlessness."[39] Of course, I don't intend to suggest that these *Memorien* influenced Kafka in any way. More simply, his consistently declared interest for the book is evidence of his sympathy and complicity with the sentiments expressed by this free and insubordinate woman. This sympathy illuminates the 1915 parable in a surprising way.

The dilemma of fear/insubordination in the face of the guardians of the Law appears also in another parable, "The Problem of Our Laws," where a people is ruled by a small group of nobles who keep the secrets of the laws even as they hold themselves above them. The conclusion is at once paradoxical and ironic: "Any party which would repudiate, not only all belief in the laws, but the nobility as well, would have the whole people behind it; yet no such party can come into existence, for nobody would dare to repudiate the nobility."[40]

It would be interesting to draw up a parallel between the man from the country and Joseph K., the hero of *The Trial*. The latter is not as passive as the former, but he also lets himself be intimidated at two decisive moments of the story. The first time comes at the beginning of the novel, when he has the intuition, at the moment that he is being arrested, that "the simplest solution to his whole story" would be to fool the guardians, to open "the door to the next room or even the door to the ante-chamber" and thus to escape to freedom. He ends up resigning himself because he worries about the reaction of the inspectors, "preferring the certainty of the solution that the natural course of things would necessarily bring." Well, we know what the necessary end to the "natural course of things" turns out to be: the execution of Joseph K. at the end of his labyrinthine path through the judicial process. His execution is his second, and final, moment of resignation: as we saw, rather than resisting his torturers, he "acquiesces" to their infamous task and ends up dying "like a dog." The man from the country in the parable is not explicitly described as a dog, but the image is strongly suggested by the degradation of his behavior: he no longer speaks, he growls; he no longer addresses the guardian but rather the fleas in the collar of his coat.

The doorkeepers of the Law, like the judges in *The Trial*, the officials in *The Castle*, and the commanders from "In the Penal Colony," do not in any way, in Kafka's eyes, represent divinity (or its servants, angels, messengers, etc.). They are precisely the representatives of the world of nonliberty, of nonredemption, of the suffocating world from which God has withdrawn. In the face of their arbitrary, petty, and unjust authority, the only road to salvation would be to follow one's own *individual* law, refusing submission and traversing the barriers of prohibition. Only in this way can one accede to divine Law, whose light is hidden behind the door.

Several passages in the *Diaries* suggest that for Kafka the crossing of the threshold or the act of "forcing the door" is a sort of allegory for individual self-affirmation and freedom. According to a fragment of a 1911 narrative, "simply crossing the threshold" is a sort of categorical imperative: "It's only in this way that one is behaving as one should in relation to oneself and to the world." In another entry, where the writer speaks in the first person (November 6, 1913), the traversing of "all the doors" is a synonym for audacity and self-confidence: "Whence the sudden confidence? If it would only remain! If I could go in and out of every door in this way, a passably erect person."[41] Finally, in an entry from January 20, 1915, the passive attitude of "lying down quietly and taking things in" is opposed to the active one of "forcibly entering into the world."[42]

For Kafka, the arrival of the Messiah seems directly linked to this individualist conception of faith as a "religion of liberty." In a strange aphorism dated November 30, 1917, he writes: "The Messiah will come as soon as the most unbridled individualism (*der zügelloseste Individualismus des Glaubens*) is possible in faith—as soon as nobody destroys this possibility and nobody tolerates that destruction, that is, when the graves open."[43] This amazing religious anarchism—to employ a concept dear to Gershom Scholem—informs another messianic entry from December 4, 1917: "The Messiah will come only when he is no longer needed, he will come only one day after his arrival, he will not come on the last day, but on the last day of all."[44]

Drawing together these two aphorisms, one can formulate the following hypothesis: for Kafka, messianic redemption will be the work of human beings themselves, in the moment that, following their own internal law, they will force the collapse of constraints and external authorities; the coming of the Messiah would be only the religious sanction of human self-redemption; at the very least that redemption would be the preparation, the precondition for the messianic era of absolute freedom. This position, which of course is very far from Jewish orthodoxy, has affinities with that of Buber, Benjamin, and Rosenzweig on the dialectic between human emancipation and messianic redemption.

According to Martin Buber, for example, The central theology of Judaism (unformulated and not part of dogma though at the basis of all doctrine and prophecy) is the belief in human participation in the work of redeeming the world: Human generations have a "cooperative power" and an active messianic power (*messianische Kraft*).[45] As for Franz Rosenzweig, he insists, in *The Star of Redemption*, on the fact that "the great works of liberation," inspired by the love of liberty, equality, and fraternity, constitute the "necessary conditions" for the coming of the Kingdom of God.[46]

In order to understand Kafka's spirituality as it is expressed in a paradoxical but startling form in the parable *Before the Law*, one would also have to situate it within the general frame of the "crisis of tradition" of Central European Judaism. As there existed, according to Leszek Kolakowsky, many "Christians without Church," many Jews of German culture were "(religious) Jews without Synagogue." Rather than speaking of "secularization" in the strict sense, it seems to me that one should speak of an ethical internalization of religion. As Max Weber insists in his study of the forms of religious refusal of the world, "The more a religion of salvation has been systematized and internalized in the direction of an ethic of ultimate ends (*Gesinnungsethik*), the greater becomes its tension with the world." On the other hand, as long as religion remains ritualized and legalistic, this tension appears in a "less consistent fashion."[47]

In Kafka—as with other Jewish intellectuals of Central Europe, removed from ritual and the Law, but integrated into the Jewish religious culture—the refusal of the world in the name of an "ethic of conviction," by which we mean here absolute liberty, is the form that an internalized religious sensibility takes.

F. Rosenzweig,
the necessary conditions

CHAPTER 5

THE CASTLE

Bureaucratic Despotism and Voluntary Servitude

Like all of Kafka's unfinished novels, *Das Schloss* is a strange and enigmatic literary document that causes perplexity and inspires different,
contradictory, and dissonant interpretations. Like *The Trial*, it has
been the object of a multitude of religious and theological readings;
the most influential "positive" reading of the religious dimension of
this work has been that of Max Brod.

In his famous afterword to the first edition of *The Castle* (1926),
Brod boldly claims that "this 'castle' into which Kafka cannot obtain
the right to enter and which he cannot even approach in the right
way" is "precisely 'grace' in the theological sense, the divine government (*göttliche Lenkung*) that rules over human destiny (the village). . . . *The Trial* and *The Castle* would thus present us with the two
ways—justice and grace—through which (according to the kabbalah)
divinity reveals itself to us." Even those episodes of the novel that represent the high personages of the Castle in a formidably sordid light
(e.g. the obscene letter that Sortini addresses to Amalia) are inter-
preted by Brod as a demonstration of the "incommensurability between earthly and divine action" and the "gap between human understanding and divine grace."[1] There is no point insisting on the
inadequacy of this type of reading, already rejected by Benjamin as
indefensible and more and more rejected by critics.

Far from appearing as the symbol of divine grace, as Brod would have it, the Castle seems rather to represent an infernal logic. Erich Heller rightly observes that one finds in Kafka simultaneously the dream of absolute liberty and the awareness of terrible servitude: from this irreconcilable combination comes "the conviction of damnation," which is "all that remains of faith." However, Heller is wrong in thinking that one can find in Kafka a Gnostic Manichaeanism, to the extent that the Castle of the novel would be something like "the heavily fortified garrison of a company of Gnostic demons, successfully holding up an advanced position against the maneuvers of an impatient soul."[2]

Nothing suggests that Kafka subscribed to Gnostic doctrines, and this type of interpretation—like those that refer to the kabbalah—implies an allegorical reading that is mystical and quite external to the text, one that is also unconnected to the knowledge or preoccupations of the author (one can know these through his letters, the *Diaries*, etc.). Kafka's religiosity manifests itself less by an elaborate and occult system of symbolic figures than by a certain *Stimmung*, a spiritual atmosphere, a feeling about the world and the modern human condition.

As Günter Anders correctly observed, "Kafka is neither a manipulator of allegories nor a symbolist." However Anders fails to resist the temptation of a Gnostic interpretation of Kafka's work, in particular *The Castle*. His reading mixes an extraordinary perspicacity with serious misunderstandings, and tries to interpret the author's religious ideas as follows: "In fact, what is revived in Kafka is a Marcionist idea according to which God the creator is a 'demigod' and hence 'wicked'—this parallel is all the more surprising in that in Marcion, this God-as-creator (in opposition to God-as-love) is at the same time the God of 'Law,' of the Old Testament. In Kafka as well, the divine, the Law, and "wickedness" are conjoined."[3] But again nothing in the novel indicates that the "wickedness" of the officials in the Castle has anything to do with "divinity" or with the Law of the Old

Testament—not to mention the fact that Marcionist doctrines[4] have no part in the spiritual preoccupations of Kafka.

Martin Buber also writes about "Gnostic demons," but he comes closer to the religious universe of *The Castle* when he defines it as an unredeemed, infernal world (*Unerlöstheit der Welt*).[5] In point of fact, Kafka appears to agree with August Strindberg that "hell is life on earth" (a sentiment one also finds expressed in Benjamin). In one of his Zürau aphorisms he writes: "There can be knowledge of the diabolical, but no belief in it, because there cannot be more of the diabolical than there is" (*mehr teuflisches als da ist, gibt es nicht*).[6] It's precisely this desolate view of the world that sends us back to messianic aspiration. No one understood this paradoxical dialectic better than Adorno; for him in *The Castle* (and *The Trial*) our existence is presented as "hell seen from the perspective of salvation. . . . His writing represents a standpoint from which the creation appears as lacerated and mutilated as it itself conceives hell to be . . . The light-source which shows the world's crevices to be infernal is the optimal one."[7]

In the fallen world, every isolated attempt—like K's—to confront lies with truth is doomed in advance. According to Kafka, "In a world of lies the lie is not removed from the world by means of its opposite, but only by means of a world of truth"[8]—in other words, by the destruction of the existing world and its replacement by a new one. That said, the metaphor of hell does not entirely account for the atmosphere (*Stimmung*) of the novel. The prevailing mood of *The Castle* has none of the pathos of a descent into the fifth circle; it is somber and ironic. As Lukács wrote in *Theory of the Novel*, "The writer's irony is a negative mysticism to be found in times without a god. . . . Irony . . . is the highest freedom that can be achieved in a world without God."[9]

As we know, the architecture of the novel is built around three essential elements: the Castle, the village, and the land surveyor K. The Castle itself is described as "a poor kind of collection of cottages assembled into a little town . . . while it might be all built of stone, the

paint had flaked off long ago."[10] In the face of the avalanche of theological, symbolic, and allegorical interpretations, we might do well to
exercise caution: what if the Castle is not the symbol of something
else, but simply a *castle*, that is to say the seat of a terrestrial and human power?[11] In such a reading, the "Castle" would represent power,
authority, the state, set against the people, represented by the "village," a distant and arbitrary power that governs the village by a con-
catenation of bureaucrats whose behavior is grotesque, inexplicable,
and rigorously senseless. The edifice itself—the high seat of the administrative apparatus—is inaccessible and impenetrable, as the German etymology indicates: *Schloss* also translates as "lock."

This power is not, as has been often suggested, that of an archaic
despotism like that of the Austro-Hungarian Empire. What interests
Kafka is not the traditional and personal embodiment of authority:
Count Westwest, the owner of the castle, is a negligible character in
the novel. What Kafka questions (like the anarchists) is rather the
despotic foundation of the modern state, with its bureaucratic apparatus, hierarchical and impersonal, authoritarian and alienating. And
he does this with his favorite weapon: irony, or, more precisely *black
humor*, in the surrealist sense of the term, which is one of the essential dimensions of this unfinished work.

How does the administrative system of power work? It's a structure that considers itself to be perfect and infallible: the official Bürgel
states: "Our administrative organization is faultless (*lückenlos*)." This
doesn't keep it from being irrational. In the fifth chapter, Kafka
sketches a tragicomic parody of the bureaucratic universe and of this
"official" confusion that K. calls a "ridiculous imbroglio" (*lächerliches
Gewirre*)—yet this imbroglio decides the fate of individuals. The internal logic of this system, circular and empty, is revealed by the
mayor: "Only a complete stranger would ask your question. Are there
supervisory authorities? There are only supervisory authorities. To be
sure, they're not intended to detect mistakes in the vulgar sense of the
word, since there are no mistakes, and even if there is a mistake, as in
your own case, who's to say that it's really a mistake in the long run?"[12]

The mayor thus suggests that the whole of the bureaucratic machine is composed only of supervisors who supervise one another. But he adds right away that there is nothing to supervise, since there are no real errors. Each sentence negates the previous one, and the result is an administrative "nonsense." Kafka's ironic viewpoint is that of someone who is familiar with bureaucratic language and who cruelly "deconstructs" it.

During all this time, in the background, something is developing, growing without limits, and it ends up submerging everything: the papers of officialdom, red tape, *Kanzleipapier*, this paper out of which, according to Kafka, the chains of tortured humanity are forged. The mayor's hall is filled with an ocean of paper. A mountain of paper rises in Sortini's office. A piece of paper—the files about K.—makes several round-trips between the departments A and B, which exchange volleys until the file is finally lost in the paper labyrinth of the Castle. This seems like a malicious parody of the extremely efficacious "distinction between spheres of competence" so vaunted by Max Weber.

What is the point of these innumerable files, these infinite dossiers, these protocols that stuff the closets? The official Momus admits, as he imperiously demands information from the land surveyor in order to fill out a form, that Klamm never even reads these protocols! These *Kanzleipapiere* are not means, but ends in themselves: the purpose of any form, is, in the final analysis, the form itself.[13]

The culminating point of bureaucratic alienation is achieved when the mayor describes the official apparatus as an autonomous machine, an automaton that dispenses with human participation: "It's as if the official mechanism could no longer stand up to the tension and the years of attrition caused by the same factor, which in itself may be slight, and has made the decision of its own accord with no need for the officials to take a hand."[14] Kafka describes a sort of bureaucratic *perpetuum mobile*, an administrative apparatus that makes itself autonomous and that circles around itself in the void.[15] With subtle humor, he thus presents the bureaucratic system as a reified world, in which relations between individuals become a thing, an independent object, a blind meshing of gears. We are here at the heart of modernity, in its most impersonal and mechanical guise.[16] If one compares the representation of the bureaucratic system in *The Castle* to that of contemporary sociologists like Max and Alfred Weber, one notices some similarities, but above all significant differences. Several commentators have remarked upon the similarity between the bureaucracy of the Kafkaesque castle and that described by Max Weber (an author whom Kafka surely never read): functional hierarchy, strict distribution of spheres of competence, systematic written registers, and precise regulations. However, in the opinion of José Maria Gonzalez García, the author of the most profound study of the "elective affinities" between Weber and Kafka, the differences are more important that the similarities. To begin with, Weber, unlike Kafka, was a nationalist-imperialist who supported a strong state (*Machtstaat*) in Germany. He was also convinced of the rationality and efficacy of the bureaucratic system, even if, in certain individual cases, he expresses anxiety about the threat posed by the total bureaucratization of the world.[17] Among the writings of Max Weber that are closest to Kafka's antibureaucratic sensibility, one can cite his contribution to the meetings in 1909 in Vienna of the Association for Social Politics: "This passion for bureaucracy is enough to make us despair. . . . The question is not to know how to promulgate and stimulate this evolution, but rather how to oppose this mechanism in order to keep a parcel of humanity free of this spiritual fragmentation, of this supreme domination of the bureaucratic way of life."[18]

The case of Alfred Weber (Max's younger brother) is different in the sense that Kafka knew him personally: the German sociology professor had presided over the committee that awarded Kafka his doctorate in law at the University of Prague in 1906. It's not improbable that Kafka could have read Alfred Weber's article "The Bureaucrat," published in 1910 in the journal *Neue Rundschau*, to which he subscribed. There are echoes of this article in Kafka's writings: for instance, Alfred Weber expresses concern about the "coming era of bureaucracy" and denounces bureaucracy as "a gigantic apparatus (*Apparat*) that is rising up in our lives," a "dead mechanism," monotonous and boring, that suppresses the independence of individuals, has a limitless appetite for authority, and is the object of a veritable idolatry (*Götzendienst vor dem Beamtentum*).[19] This last remark makes one think of a character like Klamm, who is revered by some of the villagers almost as a religious figure. But there too, one is struck by the differences: while Alfred Weber is concerned above all for the middle and upper classes who are condemned to the bureaucratic profession, Kafka is interested in the outcasts and other pariahs ground to pieces by the gigantic bureaucratic machine. Kafka's approach is therefore original and unique; his way of perceiving the functioning of the "apparatus" is closer to that of simple individuals lost in the bureaucratic labyrinth than to that of the sociologists, even where they are critical.

In the eyes of K., the Castle is as inaccessible as is the Tribunal for Joseph K. in *The Trial*. For the land surveyor as well as for most of the inhabitants of the village, the officials are distant and unattainable. Their behavior is cold and impersonal: Bürgel states that the officials' assessments should have no regard for the "sufferings and sorrows" of the members of the public; they dedicate themselves only to the "iron observance and performance of their duty."[20] The only "human" relations they have with the villagers are the sexual ones—in the crudest sense of the term—that they impose on the female population. This feature, which recalls the ancient lords' right of the first night, is one of the rare "premodern" elements of the novel—unless Kafka wanted to suggest that the sexual exploitation of women is perfectly compatible with the most rational and modern administrative hierarchy. In any case, in *The Castle*, he paints a picture of brutal and oppressive masculine domination over women that has few equivalents in the literature of the time. In writing that "Klamm treats women like a military commander (*Kommandant*)," who uses their bodies as he pleases,[21] he seems to suggest a parallel between this patriarchal system and military or colonial authority; he uses here the same term that designates the higher authority in the story "In the Penal Colony."[22]

Apparently, these sexual practices are in contradiction with the impersonal nature of administrative functions. But in fact, the relations between the officials and the women are not personal ones in the strict sense: they are treated like interchangeable figures and simple objects of sexual appetite. There is no question of love or of any personal connection between Klamm and Gardena, the landlady: after having summoned her three times to his bed, the official stops calling her and completely forgets her. In the discourse of some bureaucrats, sexuality is evoked only as an element that can facilitate or impede the smooth functioning of the administrative apparatus. Thus, Sortini is irritated because the sight of Amalia excited him and prevented him from dedicating himself to his work. He thus sends her the order to come to the inn, and quickly too, because as a conscientious administrator he has only a half hour for the satisfaction of his sexual needs. Similarly, it is not Klamm who demands the return of his ex-mistress Frieda to the bar, but the secretary Erlanger, who is trying to avoid anything that could disturb this high official in his work: "The slightest change on his desk, the removal of a dirty mark that has been there forever, anything like that can upset a man, and so can the arrival of a new barmaid." Reduced to the unenviable status of a "dirty mark in the desk," Frieda "must return to the bar at once." As for her new lover K., he is ordered by Erlanger to submit to the objective demands of the work of administration: "I'm told that you are living with her, so kindly make sure she comes back immediately. Personal feelings must be left out of this, that's obvious, so I am not going to enter into any further discussion of it."[23]

Unlike *The Trial*, there is no executioner in *The Castle*, and no one is put to death. Despite this the Castle imposes its domination on the village population, inspiring fear and obedience. The village wisdom is expressed by the female hotel owner who describes Klamm's secretary Momus as "a tool in Klamm's hand, and woe to him that doesn't obey him."[24] Amalia is punished because she commits the irreparable error of defying authority by refusing the advances of the official Sortini. Because of her crime of lèse-majesté Amalia, along with her entire family, is ostracized, not just by the Castle, but by all the people of the village, who treat them like pariahs or carriers of the plague. In vain, those closest to her attempt to obtain a pardon, but no form of supplication, humiliation, proof of submissiveness, or self-flagellation (for instance her sister Olga's bedding down with the officials' servants in the stables) can influence the decision of the Castle. The bureaucrats' answer to these desperate demands for pardon is a perfect example of administrative logic: there is nothing to forgive, since "no one had so far reported any wrongdoing."[25]

Analyzing what he calls the "shabbiness" in Kafka's novels, Adorno formulates one of his characteristic acerbic comments: "Kafka scrutinizes the smudges left behind in the deluxe edition of the book of life by the fingers of power."[26] The chapters on Amalia and her family are among the most poignant of the novel. The servility of the "doomed" family is impressive. But the subservience of the other inhabitants of the village who exclude them like lepers and act as though they were no longer human without any explicit order or decree from the Castle is even worse. It's completely ignominious. We are witness here to a remarkable example of voluntary servitude, in the strong sense employed by La Boétie.[27] Elias Canetti justly comments that the theme of the novel is "humiliation at the hands of the superiors (*Herrschaft*)" and adds: "No author ever wrote a clearer attack on subjection to the superior."[28]

The theme of voluntary servitude appears in several other texts of Kafka's. For example, in a story, published by Brod in the collection *Fragments from the Notebooks and Loose Pages*, one reads, "One is ashamed to say by what means the imperial colonel governs our little town in the mountains. His few soldiers could be disarmed immediately, if we so wished, and help for him, even supposing he could summon it—but how could he do that?—would not come for days, indeed for weeks. And so he is utterly dependent on our obedience . . . and so why do we tolerate his hated rule? There is no doubt about it:

only because of his gaze."[29] Like La Boétie, Kafka insists on the fact that submissiveness is the only foundation of the power of "one against all," a submissiveness that elicits, in this fragment as well as in the conclusion of *The Trial*, a feeling of shame.

One finds the colonel or his equivalent in the story "The Refusal": "A few soldiers kept watch, some of them standing around him [the colonel] in a semicircle. Actually a single soldier would have been quite enough, such is our fear of them." The colonel always responds to the humble petitions brought before him respectfully by a delegation of the people by having an underling tell them: "The petition has been refused . . . you may go." In this story, there is, however, a slight difference: "There is, so far as my observations go, a certain age group that is not content—these are the young people between seventeen and twenty. Quite young fellows, in fact, who are utterly incapable of foreseeing the consequences of even the least significant, far less a revolutionary idea. And it is among just them that discontent creeps in."[30] In both texts, it is a question of a tyrannical, personal, and pre-modern power founded on tradition. In *The Castle*, on the other hand, as we have seen, the power is bureaucratic, modern, impersonal, and "administrative." However, the submissive behavior of the "inferior" is completely analogous in both cases.

In a commentary on the villagers the land surveyor K. does not hesitate to criticize this self-enslavement: "Awe of the authorities is innate in all of you here, and then it is also dinned into you throughout your lives in all manner of different ways and from all sides, and you yourselves add to it as best you can."[31] Who then is this K., this would-be land surveyor who dares to criticize the servile behavior of the inhabitants? No one says it better than the landlady, who is not exactly fond of him: "You're not from the castle, you're not from the village, you're nothing. Unfortunately, however, you *are* a stranger, a superfluous person getting in everyone's way, a man who is always causing trouble."[32] Is this a reference to the Jew, who is always a stranger, an eternal bother, always "in the way?" As previously mentioned, this is Hannah Arendt's position. Though the Jewish condition may have inspired Kafka's invention of the character, it's clear that he represents a *universal* figure: the foreigner, the immigrant, the one who belongs to nothing, who comes from nowhere, the *Aussenseiter* or outsider, at the margins of established institutions and social structures. In his commentary on Kafka, whom he calls "the most lucid of universal strangers," Zygmunt Bauman considers the stranger, who is always the sole hero of his novels, the universal archetype because of his rootlessness, his lack of a home or "natural" place.[33]

Yet the land surveyor is not just any stranger: he is someone who dares to express criticism and who, with supreme insolence, claims to have rights—someone, in short, who refuses voluntary servitude. As soon as he arrives in the village, he does not hesitate to defy the authorities, dismissing the young and arrogant official Schwarzer, who demands "respect for the count's authority." In a conversation with the landlord the same night, he sums up his existential attitude in a few words: "I always prefer to be a free agent." Admittedly, this sentence is intended to explain his refusal to live in the Castle, but it's import is much more general: it can be said that it perfectly describes the behavior of the character. Of course, he is not a rebel: he is only asking for the recognition of his functions as a surveyor. But he does not share in the least degree the timorous and submissive attitude of the village inhabitants. For example, he explains to the landlord his conduct toward the powerful as follows: "I'm not of the timid sort myself, and I can speak my mind even to a count, but of course it's far better to be on friendly terms with such gentlemen."[34] What he wants from the authorities in the Castle is the universal demand of all the outcasts and pariahs of modern societies: "I don't want any tokens of favor (*Gnadengeschenke*) from the castle, I want my rights (*mein Recht*).[35] But this is precisely what is denied him, in the name of an interminable list of "administrative" reasons that make him indignant: "My very existence . . . is threatened by a disgraceful official organization (*schmachvolle amtliche Wirtschaft*)."[36]

K. does not feel the need to take up the cause of the villagers or to organize a collective action: "He didn't want to be welcomed as a man who brings happiness; . . . whoever did that was leading him astray and trying to force him into a role that he was unwilling to assume, even with the best will in the world."[37] His attitude is at the same time defensive and combative, but also strictly individualistic: "I and perhaps the law too have been shockingly abused. Personally, I will know how to defend myself."[38] Alas, as he finds out, the individual is impotent in the face of the obscure and omnipotent bureaucratic apparatus.

The land surveyor considers his relation to this apparatus "a struggle," a difficult combat in which he is forced to acknowledge the "disproportionate balance of power between the authorities and himself."[39] His defiant attitude toward the representatives of the Castle surprises and shocks the villagers, who try to offer him advice about prudence and submissiveness. The landlady complains that he never stops "saying no, no, all the time" and that he relies only on his own mind (*auf seinen Kopf schwört*), and that he ignores advice made with the best intentions.[40] As for the mayor, the teacher tells K., "The village mayor fears that, if the decision on your affairs is too long in coming, you may do something thoughtless of your own accord (*auf eigene Faust*)."[41] The German expressions *auf seinen Kopf* (literally "his own head") and *auf eigene Faust* are precise indicators of K.'s individualist, independent, and rebellious spirit.

It is therefore not surprising that he reacts with indignation upon hearing "Amalia's secret" and the reasons for her ostracism. Her sister Olga describes the event with a sort of sad resignation, while K. exclaims, "Surely Amalia couldn't be prosecuted or actually punished for Sortini's criminal behavior." This protest gives rise to Olga's resigned comment: "It seems to you unjust and monstrous, but that is not the general opinion of the village."[42] There could be no better way to demonstrate the abyss that separates the autonomous reasoning of the land surveyor—an individual who swears only by himself (*auf seinen Kopf*)—and the general submissiveness. In a passage that the author crossed out, Olga expresses her admiration for K., an individual come from elsewhere who does not share the villagers' fears: "You are amazing . . . you see everything at a glance . . . no doubt it's because you come from outside. We, on the other hand, the people from here with their sad experiences and their constant scares, we cannot resist our fears; we are afraid if we even hear the wood creaking . . . how lucky for us that you came."[43]

Before the Castle and its officials, Kafka finds himself in a situation analogous to that of the man from the country who arrives before the doorkeeper of the Law in the parable from *The Trial*. One finds the echo of this in a suggestive passage: "K. had spoken as if he were at Klamm's own door and addressing the doorkeeper."[44] However, unlike the character in the parable, the land surveyor is not afraid of violating prohibitions and confronting obstacles: in the Castle, he explains to Olga, "If it is an anteroom there are doors leading further, barriers that can be crossed if you know how to do it."[45] Thus, in one of the last chapters of the unfinished novel, he enters the corridors of the officials without authorization and greatly disturbs the services: "Neither the landlord nor the landlady understood how K. could have done anything of the kind."[46] In this way, K. represents the antithesis of "the man from the country" who waits an entire lifetime in vain, patient and submissive, hoping to be admitted to the doors of the Law. On the other hand, one finds characters in *The Castle* who resemble the antihero of the parable to a surprising degree: for instance Olga describes a person who might wait patiently for years to enter into service with the Castle: "After many years, perhaps in old age, he learns that all is lost and his life has been in vain."[47]

Why don't the authorities punish the land surveyor? They content themselves with playing a cat-and-mouse game with him, until he dies of "exhaustion"—the probable conclusion of the novel, according to Max Brod's reported conversation with the author. It's a question that is not directly addressed in the text. One can suppose that the powers of the Castle consider this individual insurrectional campaign impotent and inoffensive as well as incapable of having any sort of influence on the submissive and obedient village population.

According to Marthe Robert, the land surveyor K. represents a new stage (after Joseph K. and *The Trial*) in "the hero's slow progress toward the reconquest of his 'self' from the tyranny of the 'administrative apparatus'": he dies exhausted, but he at least has the satisfaction of "having dismantled, piece by piece, symbol by symbol, sign by sin, the all-powerful edifice, which remains standing thanks only to the despotism of the masters, duly supported by the mental laziness and credulity of the blinded subjects."[48] The land surveyor is the stranger who finds himself outside the relation of dominance-submissiveness between the Castle and the village. As a stranger, he is able to be astonished—in the sense of Greek *thaumasein*, the origin of all philosophical inquiry—when confronted with the bureaucratic absurd incarnated by the Castle officials.

How can we explain this "new phase?" Why does the theme of resistance to power take a much larger place in *The Castle* than in *The Trial*, whose dramatic conclusion seems to confirm the fatalistic resignation of its victims? A possible explanation might be the distinct historical conjunctions during the writing of the two novels. In 1914–1915, in the first years of the war, European consciousness is largely dominated by conformism, whereas the years 1918–1922 give rise in Central Europe (Germany and the Austro-Hungarian Empire) to the greatest insurrectional wave of the twentieth century. While the topic of *The Castle* is in no sense revolution or collective rebellion, the theme of individual insubordination is an essential dimension of the novel.

Is the stranger the only one not to bow down before the powerful? Such is the opinion of numerous commentators, including some of the most lucid ones, like Hannah Arendt: "Because he insists on human rights, the stranger shows himself to be the only one who would still has a conception of simple human life (*einem einfach menschlichem Leben*) in the world."[49] However, an attentive reading of the novel shows that the land surveyor K. is not the only critical, protesting, or rebellious voice in *The Castle*. The little servant Pepi, for example, who had replaced Frieda for a few days at Castle Inn, confides in K. and tells him her fondest dream, a real dream of anarchist revolt:

"If there was a man with the strength of mind to set fire to the whole Castle Inn and burn it to the ground, leaving no trace, like a piece of paper in the stove, he would be the man of Pepi's dreams today."[50] This pronouncement echoes one of Kafka's own, as reported by Max Brod: Kafka was surprised that workers confronted by the maneuvers of the administration to deny them their social benefits and disability payments did not attack and tear down the building.

There is another character who doesn't bow down, someone who doesn't limit herself to dreaming like Pepi and whose insubordination is much more dramatic than that of the land surveyor K.; unlike the other villagers, she "doesn't know the meaning of fear" and proves herself capable of "heroic acts" against the authorities.[51] This is Amalia, a woman of the people whose sad, proud, and sincere glance, like her words, is characterized by a sort of "pride" that does not fail to impress K. In chapter 17, we learn "Amalia's secret": having received from the crude and arrogant official Sortini a "vulgar"—in other words, obscene—message ordering her to come to him at Castle Inn, she immediately tears it up and throws the scraps of paper into the face of the messenger sent by the man of the Castle. It's an apparently harmless act, but in reality it represents unheard-of courage. As Olga states, "Very likely no official was ever rejected in those terms before."[52] If the official's attempt failed, it's because, as K. says, he found in Amalia "a stronger opponent,"[53] at least from the point of view of moral and spiritual strength. This was enough to expose her along with her whole family to the malediction of the higher orders, who decisively and irrevocably ostracize them.[54]

Amalia is one of the rare characters in the novels of Kafka who resolutely incarnates disobedience, insubordination, and, in short, human dignity—and who pays the highest price for it. She demonstrates that in the very midst of the village, among the "common people" (not only in the case of strangers from outside) there are those who possess the resources of courage, pride, and resistance. To be sure, she is an exceptional character, who willfully detaches herself from the sheeplike mass of the villagers, but she does exist. Is it by chance that she happens to be a woman?[55] One wonders whether the model for this literary figure might be Kafka's favorite sister Ottla, whom he describes, in the "Letter to My Father," as having "a Löwy's defiance, sensitivity, restlessness, and a sense of justice" and whom he enormously admired for being "more confident, self-trusting, healthy, and unhesitant . . . compared to me."[56]

For some reason, the majority of critics have had their eyes fixed on the character of the land surveyor and have neglected Amalia, who is without a doubt one of the most impressive female figures in Kafka's entire oeuvre. She is a figure who embodies, in exemplary fashion, the antiauthoritarian individualism of the author.

CHAPTER 6

ANECDOTAL DIGRESSION
Was Kafka a Realist?

Neither Adorno, nor Benjamin, nor Karel Kosik—and certainly not André Breton!—addressed the question of Kafka's realism. It's a subject that has not attracted the attention of critical Marxists. On the other hand, in the "post-Stalinist" Communist movement, the debate essentially concentrated on this serious inquiry: was the author of *The Trial* a "realist" writer or not?

Georg Lukács stands out by taking the strongest negative position. Of course, we are not talking here about the revolutionary philosopher of *History and Class Consciousness* (1923), but of the late Lukács who had been marked by Stalinism. In one of his worst books, *The Meaning of Contemporary Realism* (written in 1955), the Hungarian intellectual compares Kafka to Thomas Mann in order to emphasize the lack of realism—and therefore irrelevance for leftist culture—in the former. His point of departure is at the same time incredibly narrow and completely arbitrary: Lukács considers the peace movement—sponsored at the time by the USSR—as the standard for judging all of twentieth-century literature. He separates "bourgeois" intellectuals and writers into two categories: those who take part in the peace movement and those in whom "a belief in the inevitability of war . . . is often rooted in philosophical fatalism."[1]

Then, with extraordinary superficiality, he claims to discern two pairs of contrasting elements, on the one hand realism versus antirealism (which he equates with the avant-garde and with decadence), and on the other, the choice between war and peace.[2] In this little master-piece of Stalinist casuistry, Kafka becomes the extreme expression of decadent avant-gardism that refuses to fight for peace. For Lukács in 1955, the choice between Thomas Mann and Kafka is equivalent to the choice between health and social illness, or between a true-to-life critical realism and an artistically interesting decadence.[3] This opin-ion was apparently shared by the Czech Stalinist bureaucracy, for whom the name of Kafka was taboo, and which refused to publish this heretical author.[4]

In examining the principal works of Kafka, Lukács sees nothing more than the product of a purely subjectivist vision of the world, according to which "the realistic detail is the expression of a ghostly un-reality, of a nightmare world, whose function is to evoke *Angst*" and in which "the world is an allegory of transcendent nothingness."[5]

Lukács's criticism is evidence of a strange blindness: he does not understand that this absence of content, this elusive sphere and tran-scendence, do not refer to a "nothingness," but to the very structure of reification—as he had himself studied in his remarkable *History and Class Consciousness*—as well as to, more concretely, the abstract, empty, elusive, and transcendent impersonality of an alienated and reified bureaucracy. The literary output that Lukács dismissed as "anti-realist" has contributed, perhaps more than any other in the twentieth century, to a critical awareness of the political realities of the modern world.[6]

Lukács seems, however, to have revised his opinion. Here is a curious story that he told his Hungarian disciples: after the Soviet invasion and the fall of the Hungarian Republic Workers' Councils presided over by Imre Nagy in 1956, Nagy and his ministers—among them Lukács, as minister of culture—were interned in a for-tress somewhere in Romania while awaiting to be judged. Since they had no access to the indictment, they had no idea what crimes they were accused of and found it impossible to defend themselves. They did not know what kind of tribunal was supposed to judge them: Hungarian magistrates? The new party heads? The Soviet Politburo? Or simply a mixture of Hungarian and Russian political police? Some months later, a few left for their executions—among them Imre Nagy—while others, like Lukács, were set free thanks to doubts about their guilt. It seems that one day, during this long and anxious waiting period, the philosopher turned to his wife during a walk in the courtyard and said: *Kafka war doch ein Realist* (So Kafka was a realist after all!).[7]

In any case, in the following years—perhaps under the influence of the events in Hungary in 1956—he was to radically revise his judgment of Kafka: in an essay in 1965, he outlines (without developing it) an analysis that is situated at the opposite pole of that of 1955: "Kafka ... dramatizes an entire epoch of inhumanity.... Consequently his universe ... attains a moving and profound seriousness, unlike writers who, describing the same historical foundation, try to represent the naked and abstract generalities of human existence, and infallibly end up in complete emptiness, in the void."[8]

The positions that Lukács took in 1955 were far from enjoying unanimity among intellectuals of Communist persuasion, as can be seen in the Kafka conference organized by Eduard Goldstücker in Liblice, Czechoslovakia, in 1963—with the participation of Ernst Fischer, Anna Seghers, Klaus Hermsdorf and Roger Garaudy, as well as Czech, Polish, Hungarian, Yugoslavian, and East German specialists.[9]

Without doubt the contribution by the remarkable Austrian philosopher and literary historian Ernst Fischer was the most interesting. Responding to Lukács's argument, he states; "Poetry is often ahead of prose ... much of what is criticized as weakness in Kafka is on the contrary a component of his poetic power. [Thomas Mann's] *Buddenbrooks* did not penetrate so deeply into the darkness of the late capitalist world as the fragmentary novel *The Trial*. Thomas Mann reports on bourgeois development retrospectively (without an understanding of the working class); Kafka looks ahead and discovers in today's specificities the inferno of tomorrow."[10]

Fischer approaches the discussion of realism by subverting the concept of "reality," which dogmatic thinkers limit to the external world: "Aren't the various ways in which the outer world becomes a subjective experience an important aspect of reality? Is reality only what people do and what is done to them, or is it not also what they dream, suspect, and feel as not yet existing or existing only invisibly—what their anticipation includes in the here and now?"[11] And, responding to those who complain about Kafka's "negativism": "The writer is not obligated to suggest solutions. His question marks are often richer in content than frequent and too boldly printed exclamation marks."[12]

The participants at the Liblice conference congregated around two poles: on the one hand, there were those who defended the Prague writer and were energetically represented by Ernst Fischer, and also by many of the Czech participants, such as Eduard Goldstücker, Jiri Hajek, and Alexey Kusak (both of the latter referred to Karel Kosik), as well as the Pole Roman Karst and others; and on the other hand, those who criticized Kafka as a "subjectivist," namely the East Germans Klaus Hermsdorf (despite his interesting book on Kafka), Helmut Richter, and Ernst Schumacher. Roman Karst responded with irony to the eminent specialists who recommended that one read Kafka reasonably—"how in the world can one read a poet reasonably?"

What was at stake was much more than a purely literary question. For the Communists advocating "renewal," Kafka's oeuvre constitutes not only a radical critique of the negative character of the capitalist world, but also, beyond the grave, a critique of the crimes of Stalinism. Once again, it's Fischer who dots the *i*'s: the executioners who knock on Joseph K.'s door to take him to the place of execution had a great future before them in the century to come: "Kafka was no longer alive when these men, like the horsemen of the apocalypse, ranged throughout the world—and unfortunately not only through the capitalist world." He was seconded by other (especially Czech) contributors. Jiri Hajek commented, "Kafka condemns everything that stands in direct contradiction to the humanistic historical mission of socialism, everything that the Stalinist deformation brought down upon us and all of its consequences that still survive among us and in us."[13]

The mistrust on the part of the defenders of the system was not unjustified: the 1963 Liblice conference was, in the general opinion, one of the important shifts in the cultural and political climate that led, a few years later, to the Prague Spring of 1968. Thus Kafka not only contributed to an understanding and interpretation of reality, but also to transforming it in a crucial moment of the modern history of his own country.

Let us return to the question of "realism." As Ernst Fischer sarcastically noted in his 1963 talk, "God created things and the Devil created categories; only the mediocre fits into categories; the unusual bursts them."[14] The writings of Kafka, an unconventional writer to the highest degree, explodes the classical canon of literary realism, if only by their strange oneiric atmosphere.

This doesn't mean that the works have no relation to reality: something like the communicating vessels that the surrealists write about seems to connect the two spheres of waking and dreaming. Or one should rather say that Kafka erases—silently, discretely, imperceptibly—any frontier between dream and reality. One need think only of Kafka's story of a man's dream about "an ancient knight's sword" that is "buried to the hilt in his back." When he wakes up, the sword is there and has to be removed carefully, inch by inch, by his friends standing on a chair.[15] Of course in Kafka's case, unlike the surrealists, the dream is most often a nightmare.

In fact, some of his writings—the short stories and parables more than the novels—could be described as examples of "critical irrealism" rather than of realism. One finds this also in gothic novel, in tales of the fantastic, in literary utopias, and in surrealism. All of them create imaginary worlds that are ruled by the logic of the marvelous, which does not try to reproduce or represent reality but which

critical irrealism

nonetheless contains a radical critique of the real—ferocious or ironic, as the case may be.

"Realist" or not, the oeuvre of Kafka is one of the most remarkable examples in literature of what Walter Benjamin called *profane illumination*, thanks to its attitude of *permanent deviation* from social institutions. This is why André Breton considered him, simply, as "the most important seer of the century," in the poetic sense of the term, which the surrealists borrowed from Rimbaud: a seer is the one who is able to "scrutinize the invisible and hear the inaudible (*capable d'inspecter l'invisible et d'entendre l'inouï*)."[16]

Some have taken Kafka's realism seriously enough to consider him as a sort of sociologist who expresses himself in literary form. According to Axel Dornemann, the bureaucracy of the novels is a sort of "poetic version of the Weberian model, pushed to its extreme."[17] Some German political scientists go as far as to cite his novels in their scientific bibliographies on bureaucracy, next to the writings of Max Weber and other sociologists.[18] More subtle, but just as problematic, is the publication of extracts from *The Castle* by the sociologist Lewis Coser in his collection *Sociology through Literature*. In his introduction to the chapter on bureaucracy, which also includes passages from Balzac, Dickens, and other writers, Coser states: "By stressing the pathology of bureaucratic behavior, he aimed at representing in emblematic forms the nightmare of a fully rationalized world. Kafka's work can be read on many levels; the interest here is in his acute comprehension of the dysfunctional aspects of bureaucracy and in his realization that, to paraphrase Robert K. Merton, rules originally conceived as a means may become, if rigidly adhered to, transformed into ends in themselves, so that an instrumental value becomes a terminal value."[19] His remarks are interesting, but the sociological concepts "pathology," "dysfunctional," and so on, ignore the fact that Kafka's irony is directed against "normal" and "functional" procedures of the bureaucratic apparatus.

Kafka remains "untranslatable" into the language of sociology or political science. Marthe Robert is right to insist on this point: in treating the writings of Kafka as "a kind of science, or of applied religion or philosophy, one commits a grave injustice to poetic creation, which is betrayed as soon as it is translated—it cannot be reduced to any other form of expression."[20] In other words, it's with its own means of expression that literature, like poetry, is able to "view the invisible" and thus to widen our awareness of the world and of human beings.

If social science formulates concepts, laws, and analyses, the literary work makes individuals, characters, and situations come alive. If the former follows the logic of scientific rationality, the second follows the logic of imagination and produces an "effect of consciousness" that is irreplaceable by illuminating, as it were from the "inside," the contours and forms of social reality. The specific contribution of the literary work is situated at the level of concrete singularity. If it is so capable of enriching our perception of social reality, it is because the light it sheds is different from that produced by scientific concepts, which are characterized, even in the most broadly conceived sociology, by a certain externality. The interior illumination, the subjective approach, makes literature an infinitely precious and profound tool of knowledge understanding—something that no work of science, no matter how adequate, can replace.

CHAPTER 7

THE "KAFKAESQUE" SITUATION

The extraordinary impact of Kafka's oeuvre on twentieth- and twenty-first-century culture is no doubt due to its "profane illumination." Commenting on *The Trial* with his characteristic sagacity, George Steiner observes, "This short novel has achieved a stature that goes beyond that of a literary classic. All along the [twentieth] century, people have recognized themselves and spontaneously referred to it. Many are those who have never read it, who perhaps have not even seen adaptations in plays, films, or TV programs, but who are familiar with the main themes and situations. . . . Kafka has become an adjective. In more than a hundred languages, the epithet "Kafkaesque" is applied to the recurrence of inhumanity and absurdity in our times."[1]

Some fictional characters have entered the language as descriptors: someone tilting at windmills is called "quixotic"; another who hesitates is a "Hamlet"; an infernal situation is "Dantesque," while "Orwellian language" distorts the truth. The same holds for Franz Kafka: after the Second World War, a new word appeared in most languages: in English *Kafkaesque*, in French *kafkaïen*, in German *kafkaesk*, in Portuguese and Spanish *kafkiano*.[2] It seems that Malcolm Lowry was the first, as early as 1936, to speak of a "perfect Kafka situation," but it appeared for the first time as an adjective in a 1947 article in the *New Yorker*, which wrote of "a Kafkaesque nightmare of blind alleys."[3]

It's not easy to describe this term that has entered dictionaries and encyclopedias: it can refer to "a nightmarish world" in which "sinister impersonal forces control human affairs" (*Twentieth Century Words*); to a "pointless, rational organization, with tortuous bureaucratic, and totalitarian procedures, into which the bewildered individual has strayed" (*Penguin Encyclopedia* 2006); to "an oppressive atmosphere" (French *Robert* dictionary); to "a mysterious, menacing, and uncanny (*unheimlich*) situation" (German *Duden* dictionary).[4] Most dictionaries emphasize the sinister aspect and neglect the ironic dimension that is an essential part of the adjective's customary usage. In point of fact, the "Kafkaesque" situation describes a variety of experiences, going from the ridiculous absurd in the daily functioning of bureaucratic institutions up to the most murderous manifestations of "administrative" power. The extensive use of "Kafkaesque" in today's speech means that the masses of Kafka readers are not mistaken and have intuitively seized upon the way that his works are *universal* and *critical*: Kafka's protest against the bureaucratic nightmare, and his subversion of it with *black humor*, which is, in André Breton's sense, a superior revolt of the mind.[5]

It's not by chance that the "Kafkaesque" has entered into current parlance: it designates an aspect of reality that social scientists tend to ignore and for which they have no pertinent concept: the oppression and absurdity of the bureaucratic reification experienced by ordinary people. In point of fact, sociology and jurisprudence have generally limited themselves to studying the bureaucratic machine "from the inside" or in relation to elites (the state, or capitalism), focusing on its "functional" or "dysfunctional" character, its "instrumental rationality," and so on.[6]

As the surrealist Michel Carrouges emphasized in 1957, "Kafka dispenses with the corporate point of view of men of the law, these educated and well-brought-up men who think they understand the why of matters pertaining to law. He considers them and the law from the point of view of the miserable masses who have to endure them, without understanding them. But since he is Kafka, he elevates this ordinarily naive ignorance to the level of a superior irony, overflowing with suffering and humor, with mystery and clairvoyance. He unmasks all the ignorance of humanity that resides in juridical knowledge as well as the human understanding that resides in the so-called ignorance of the oppressed."[7] This can be applied not only to judicial institutions, but also to the totality of hierarchical and bureaucratic machines that, in the Kafkaesque universe, hold the "miserable masses" in their grip.

One of the best discussions of the meaning of the "Kafkaesque" can be found in an essay published in 1986 by the Czech writer Milan Kundera. According to him, the term designates situations "that no other word allows us to grasp and to which neither political or social nor psychological theory gives us any key." Its principal aspects are (1) a world that is nothing but a single, huge labyrinthine institution that [the characters] cannot escape and cannot understand; (2) In the Kafkaesque world, the file . . . represents true reality, whereas man's physical existence is only a shadow cast by his file; (3) the accused does not know what he is accused of and seeks a justification for his penalty: the punishment seeks the offense.[8]

To be sure, Kundera is understandably inclined to interpret this Kafkaesque universe on the basis of his own experience of Stalinist Czech bureaucracy. But he affirms nonetheless that "the society we call democratic is also familiar with the process that bureaucratizes and depersonalizes; the entire planet has become a theater of this process."[9] I would add that it is a process that had already been under way for quite a while in Kafka's time. I would only reproach Kundera for making the Kafkaesque into an aspect of the human condition, "one fundamental possibility of man and his world."[10] Adorno had already replied to this kind of argument, which has no basis in the texts of the novels and which risks neutralizing the powerful subversive critique of his writings.

In conclusion, Kafka is much more than a "realist" writer in the habitual use of the term. What his works let us see is not "objective reality"

but something more important: the *subjective experience* of individuals confronted with "apparatuses." His novels are written *from the
point of view of the defeated,* those who are ground up in the "rational" and "impersonal" gears of the bureaucratic machine. To paraphrase Walter Benjamin, Kafka's novels rub against the overly reas-
suring image of judicial and modern state power by going *against the
grain.*

The force of the adjective "Kafkaesque" resides in its irredeemable
contamination, in the eyes of ordinary people, of the very concept of
bureaucracy. Here is what a 1969 German *Dictionary of Organizations*
regretfully notes: "The word *bureaucracy* provokes in most people a
slight feeling of anxiety. The concept comes loaded with too many
Kafkaesque associations of opacity and the uncanny (*Unheimlich-
keit*)."[11]

While Max Weber, the most incisive of the sociologists of bureaucracy, defines it as the most rational system of administration, as the
extreme expression of rationality in the exercise of power, Kafka
shows how this mutilated instrumental rationality leads to the most
perfect irrationality. The "Kafkaesque" universe that finds expression
in his novels shares in the "dialectic of reason" analyzed by Adorno
and Horkheimer—the transformation, in modern Western society, of
rationality into its opposite.

NOTES

Introduction ✓

1. Walter Benjamin, *Selected Writings*, vol. 2, *1927–1924*, trans. Rodney Livingstone, ed. Michael W. Jennings, Howard Eiland, and Gary Smith (Cambridge, MA: Harvard University Press, 1999), 804.

2. Marthe Robert, "Introduction," Franz Kafka, *Journal* (Paris: Grasset, 1954), xiv–xv.

3. Walter Benjamin, "Surrealism: The Last Snapshot of the European Intelligentsia," in *Selected Writings*, 2:215.

4. Walter Benjamin, "On the Concept of History," in *Selected Writings*, vol. 4, *1938–1940*, ed. Michael W. Jennings, trans. Edmund Jephcott et al. (Cambridge: Harvard University Press, 2003), 391.

5. Janouch, *Conversations with Kafka*, trans. Goronwy Rees (London: Quartet Books, 1985), 120 [the translation has been changed slightly].

6. Franz Kafka, *Briefe, 1902–1924*, ed. Max Brod (New York: Schocken, 1958), 27–28.

7. Annie Goldmann and Sami Nair, eds., *Essais sur les formes et leurs significations* (Paris: Médiations, 1981).

Chapter 1 ✓

1. Lucien Goldmann, "Matérialisme dialectique et histoire de la littérature," in *Recherches dialectiques* (Paris: Gallimard, 1959), 45–64.

2. [*Translator's note*: The French word *libertaire* refers to partisans of anarchist, semianarchist, or antiauthoritarian forms of *socialism*. *Libertarian*, when it appears in the translation, has obviously nothing to do with the US group of self-styled "libertarians," right-wing partisans of extreme free-

market *capitalism*, and therefore opposed to any form of state intervention, in particular welfare-state initiatives.]

3. Hugo Bergmann, "Erinnerungen an Franz Kafka," in *Exhibition Franz Kafka, 1883–1913: Catalogue* (Jerusalem: Jewish National and University Library, 1969), 8. In his remarkable biography of the young Kafka, Klaus Wagenbach comments on the gymnasium years: "The most deliberately independent act—and the one that had the most serious consequences for his subsequent life—was his sudden adhesion to socialism at the age of sixteen. . . . Socialism, which has heretofore been neglected by his biographers—was to play an important role in Kafka's life." See Klaus Wagenbach, *Franz Kafka: Eine Biographie seiner Jugend, 1883–1912* (Berlin: Klaus Wagenbach, 2006), 60.

4. Reported by Hugo Bergmann and noted by Wagenbach, *Franz Kafka*, 62. As we will see later, other witnesses (Leopold Kreitner) mention the young Kafka's "cosmopolitan socialism" and antinationalism.

5. Franz Kafka, *Briefe, 1918–1920*, ed. Hans-Gerd Koch (Frankfurt am Main: S. Fischer, 2003), 324.

6. See Franz Kafka, *Briefe an Milena*, ed. Jürgen Born and Michael Müller (Frankfurt am Main: Fischer Verlag, 1983), 348 n. 238.

7. Franz Kafka, *Letters to Milena*, trans. Tania Stern and James Stern, ed. Willi Haas (New York: Schocken, 1962), 192. See Bertrand Russell, "Soviet Russia—1920," *The Nation* 111, no. 2874 (July 31, 1920), 122–23.

8. Kafka, *Letters to Milena*, 195.

9. Russell, "Soviet Russia—1920," 123.

10. This issue is destined to be at the center of the decisive conflict in the Bolshevist party after the death of Lenin—a conflict between, on the one hand, the partisans of revolutionary internationalism (Trotsky and the left opposition) and, on the other hand, those of "socialism in one country" (Stalin and his supporters). In his book on Kafka's politics, Dušan Glišović tries to "explain" Kafka's comments on the Russian Revolution as an attempt to "give Milena the impression" that he was a communist, by "flattering" her opinions. He calls it a "way of furthering his amorous intentions through the expression of political opinions." See Dušan Glišović, *Politik im Werk Kafkas* (Tübingen: Francke Verlag, 1996), 30–31. I'm afraid I can't take this suggestion seriously. To begin with, Milena was not even communist at this time; and, as far as any one knows, Kafka never adapted his political opinions—or any others—to the taste of his correspondents!

11. Janouch, *Conversations with Kafka*, 119.

12. Unlike the Russian Revolution, the revolutionary movements of Cen-

tral Europe—Berlin, Vienna, or Budapest—did not elicit any comments from Kafka. The only exception is the short-lived Bavarian Soviet Republic, whose leaders—socialists, communists, or anarchists—were Jewish. In his letters, Kafka expresses distress over the execution of the communist Eugen Levine and the murder of the anarchist Gustav Landauer; he seems to think that the central role played by Jews in this movement was a mistake that was capable of contributing to an increase in anti-Semitism in Germany; on the other hand he has nothing but contempt for the reactionary Austrian officers he met during a meal in his pension in Meran, whom he reported as saying, "It's only the Jewish communists and socialists whom we cannot forgive; them we drown in the soup and cut up with the roast." See Franz Kafka, *Briefe, 1902–1924*, 274–75.

13. Max Brod, *Franz Kafka: A Biography*, trans. G. Humphreys Roberts and Richard Winston (New York: Schocken, 1960), 86.

14. Michal Mares, "Wie ich Franz Kafka kennenlernte," in Wagenbach, *Franz Kafka*, 271. See also Michal Mares, "Kafka und die Anarchisten," in Hans-Gerd Koch, ed., *Als Kafka mir entgegenkam* (Berlin: Verlag Klaus Wagenbach, 2005), 86–91. There is an extensive discussion of Mares's report in Wagenbach, *Franz Kafka*, 162–64.

15. Michael Mares, "Franz Kafka," unpublished ms. in Czech, no date (though later than the 1946 event that it mentions). I am grateful to M. Vaclav Tomek of the Czech Academy of Sciences and a renowned specialist in the history of Czech anarchism for having shared this document with me (translated into French by Milena Braud).

16. Janouch, *Conversations with Kafka*, 86.

17. On this point see the commentary of the Brazilian philosopher Leandro Konder in *Kafka, vida e obra* (São Paulo: Paz e Terra, 1979), 36.

18. Janouch, *Conversations with Kafka*, 151–52.

19. Ibid., 119–20 [the translation has been slightly changed].

20. Ibid., 90.

21. Max Brod, as well as Felix Weltsch and Dora Dymant, the companion of Kafka's last years, were convinced of the authenticity of the first version of Janouch's text, published in 1952. As far as I know, the most systematic criticism of Janouch's book was made by Eduard Goldstücker in 1980. Goldstücker rightly notes the error concerning the visit to the anarchists' clubs in the company of Brod. It's certainly a mistake on Janouch's part (he would only have to have reread Brod's biography of Kafka to realize his error), but Goldstücker, who wants to settle accounts with Janouch, calls it a "lie" and a "falsification." Most of his remarks are about errors in dates, such as Ja-

nouch's reports of meeting Kafka in Prague at a time when the author was in Meran. These are pertinent remarks, and one cannot deny that Janouch's book contains a lot of imprecisions, especially the second edition. But Goldstücker goes too far in saying, as he states at the beginning of his article, that both versions of the *Conversations with Kafka* are "apocryphal." Goldstücker claims that "anyone who would think that Kafka could say those things didn't know him." It's an odd statement, considering that Brod, Dymant, and Weltsch (who, unlike Goldstücker, knew Kafka) considered them authentic. See Eduard Goldstücker, "Kafkas Eckermann? Zu Gustav Janouch's 'Gespräche mit Kafka,'" in Claude David, ed., *Franz Kafka: Themen und Probleme* (Göttingen: Vandenloch & Ruprecht), 1980, 238–52. For a convincing refutation of Goldstücker's arguments see the article by Whayoung Yu-Oh, "Über die Echtheitsfrage der 'Gespräche mit Kafka' von Gustav Janouch," in *Franz Kafkas Sendungsbewusstsein* (Tübingen: Francke Verlag, 1994), 224–31.

22. Gustav Janouch, *Kafka und seine Welt* (Vienna: Hans Deutsch Verlag, 1965), 102–4. According to Janouch, Stanislas K. Neumann and Jaroslav Hasek left the clubs for these same reasons.

23. Leopold Kreitner, "Kafka as a Young Man," *Connecticut Review* 3, no. 2 (1970), 29–30. See also Koch, *Als Kafka mir entgegenkam*, 52–58. Besides the two names cited above, Kreitner mentions Frana Sramek and Stansilas K. Neumann as participants.

24. It's not possible for me, within the confines of this essay, to analyze more closely the activities, ideology, and evolution of the different aspects of Prague anarchism. I can only refer here to the magisterial study of Vaclav Tomek, *Cesky Anarchismus: A jeho publicistika 1880-1925* (Prague: Filosofia, 2002), with a summary in German and English). A shorter German version can be found in Vaclav Tomek, *Volk! Öffne Deine Augen! Skizzen zum tschechischen Anarchismus von den Anfängen bis 1925* (Vienna: Verlag Monte Verita, 1995).

25. See Wagenbach, *Franz Kafka*, 204 n. 222; and Wagenbach, *Franz Kafka in Selbstzeugnissen und Bilddokumenten* (Hamburg: Rowohlt, 1964), 70; Max Brod, *Streitbares Leben 1894–1968* (Munich: F.A. Herbig, 1969), 170; and Brod, *Franz Kafka: A Biography*, 216. See also Max Brod, *Über Franz Kafka* (Frankfurt am Main: Fischer, 1974), 190.

26. Eduard Goldstücker, "Über Franz Kafka aus der Prager Perspektive 1963," in Eduard Goldstücker et al., eds., *Franz Kafka aus Prager Sicht* (Prague: Verlag der Tschechoslowakischen Akademie der Wissenschaften, 1963), 40–45.

27. Hartmut Binder, *Kafka-Handbuch*, vol. 1, *Der Mensch und seine Zeit* (Stuttgart: Alfred Kröner, 1979), 361–62.

28. Ibid.

29. Ibid., 362–63. The idea that Kafka could be hiding certain informations from him was not surprising for Brod, who emphasizes, in his autobiography: "In contrast to me, Kafka was a closed character and did not open the access to his soul to nobody, not even to me; I knew quite well that he sometimes kept for himself important things." Max Brod, *Streitbares Leben 1884–1968*, 46–47.

30. Ibid., 364. See Kafka, *Briefe an Milena*, 306. According to Binder, "if Mares had really given him Kropotkin's *Words of a Rebel*, one would not find in his *Diaries* the following remark: "Don't forget Kropotkine!" Once more, it is difficult to see the relation between the fact mentioned by Binder and his conclusion . . .

31. Kafka, *Briefe an Milena*, 306.

32. Michal Mares, in Wagenbach, *Franz Kafka*, 271; Binder, *Kafka-Handbuch*, 363–64; Kafka, *Briefe an Milena*, editors' note, 336 n. 111.

33. Binder, *Kafka Handbuch*, 365.

34. Ernst Pawel, *The Nightmare of Reason: A Life of Franz Kafka* (New York: Farrar, Straus and Giroux, 1984), 152.

35. Ibid.

36. Ibid., 152–53. In another chapter, Pawel refers to Kafka as "a metaphysical anarchist with no talent for party politics"—a definition that seems quite pertinent to me. As for the memoirs of Janouch, Pawel considers them "plausible" but with reservations (72).

37. Ritchie Robertson, *Kafka, Judaism, Politics and Literature* (Oxford: Clarendon Press, 1985), 140.

38. Ibid., 141: "If one is inquiring into Kafka's political leanings, it is, in fact, misleading to think in terms of the usual antithesis between left and right. The appropriate context would be the ideology which Michael Löwy has labeled 'romantic anti-capitalism'. . . . Romantic anti-capitalism (to adopt Löwy's term, though 'anti-industrialism' might be more accurate), had many different versions . . . but as a general ideology is transcended by the opposition between left and right." Robertson is referring here to my first attempt to describe "romantic anti-capitalism" in a book on Lukács.

39. I tried to analyze romanticism in my book *Georg Lukacs: From Romanticism to Bolchevism*, London, Verso, 1981, quoted by Robertson. More recently I returned to the subject, with my friend Robert Sayre, in *Romanticism against the Tide of Modernity*, Durham, Duke University Press, 2001.

40. Franz Kafka, *Wedding Preparations in the Country and Other Posthumous Prose Writings*, trans. Ernst Kaiser and Eithne Wilkins (London: Secker and Warburg, 1954), 43.

41. Ibid., 39. It's interesting that Hannah Arendt compares Kafka's refusal of the idea of progress as inevitable, with the association between progress and catastrophe expressed by Walter Benjamin in the famous ninth thesis of his document "The Concept of History." See Hannah Arendt, "Franz Kafka: A Reevaluation," *Partisan Review* 11, no. 4 (1944), 417.

[handwritten margin note: Arendt on Kafka]

42. Kafka, *Briefe, 1902–1924*, 196. I will return to Otto Gross in a subsequent chapter. Kafka also knew the literary writings of Gustav Landauer, which are mentioned in his letters to Milena. See Kafka, *Briefe, April 1914–1917* (Frankfurt am Main: S. Fischer, 2005), 364.

43. Franz Kafka, *The Diaries of Franz Kafka, 1910–1913*, ed. Max Brod, trans. Joseph Kresh (New York: Schocken, 1948), 303 (entry dated October 13, 1913).

44. Petr Kropotkin, *Memoirs of a Revolutionist* (New York: Dover Publications, 1988), 51.

45. Ibid., 296–99.

46. Mares claims to have given Kafka a copy of *Words of a Rebel* (1885), another famous book by the Russian anarchist prince. One can't find this book in any known listing of Kafka's library holdings. It's not impossible that he would have read it, despite his preference for militant autobiographies rather than doctrinal expositions. In any case, some of the themes of that book share undeniable affinities with Kafka's writings, as, for instance, when Kropotkin denounces the oppression of individuals by the immense apparatus of the law and authoritarianism, with its judges, jailers, and executioners whose purpose is solely to maintain the "monopoly to the profit of a few against the whole of humanity." He writes: "The governmental machine, charged with sustaining order, has not yet completely broken down. But at each turn of its worn-out wheels, it stumbles and halts. Its functioning becomes more and more difficult, and the discontent caused by its failures steadily increases." Peter Kropotkin, *Words of a Rebel*, trans. George Woodcock (Montreal: Black Rose Books, 1992), 159 and 184.

47. Isaiah Berlin, "Introduction," in Alexander Herzen, *My Past and Thoughts: The Memoirs of Alexander Herzen* (New York: Alfred Knopf, 1973), xxv and xxxvi. According to Berlin, the main subject of his work is "the oppression of the individual; the humiliation and degradation of men by political and personal tyranny; the yoke of social custom, the dark ignorance, and savage, arbitrary misgovernment which maimed and destroyed

human beings in the brutal and odious Russian empire." He also "had a distaste for all that was centralized, bureaucratic, hierarchical, subject to rigid forms or rules" (xxiv and xxxiii).

48. Herzen, *My Past and Thoughts*, 69 and 501. The first mention of Herzen's memoirs occurs in Kafka's diaries on December 23, 1914.

49. Arthur Holitscher, *Amerika heute und morgen* (Frankfurt am Main: Fischer Verlag, 1912), 376–81.

50. Arthur Holitscher, *Lebensgeschichte eines Rebellen: Meine Erinnerungen* (Frankfurt am Main: Fischer Verlag, 1924). See Kafka, *Briefe, 1902–1924*, 478. There are other works of anarchist inspiration in Kafka's library or mentioned in his correspondence: the memoirs of Tolstoy, two books of poetry by Michal Mares, and the periodical *Wohlstand für alle* (*Prosperity for All*) edited by the Viennese anarchist Rudolf Grossmann.

51. Mahlwida von Meyseburg, *Memorien einer Idealistin*, vol. 1 (Berlin: Schuster & Loeffler, 1904), 185. It's Michal Mares who mentions that Kafka read this book. For an account of Kafka's readings in politics, see Glišović, *Politik im Werke Kafkas*, 20–27.

52. Franz Kafka, *Tagebücher* (Frankfurt am Main: Fischer Verlag, 1992), 915–23.

53. Frana Sramek, *Flammmen* (Leipzig: Ernst Rowolt Verlag, 1913). In one of his stories, a courageous young woman compares soldiers to trees that in spring are stripped of their flowers and leaves, and whose branches are broken. The woman becomes the victim of the tyrannical forces whose orders she refuses to obey (67–69).

54. Janouch, *Conversations with Kafka*, 15. See Felix Weltsch, "The Rise and Fall of the Jewish-German Symbiosis: The Case of Franz Kafka," *Yearbook of the Leo Baeck Institute*, vol. 1 (London: Leo Baeck Institute, 1956), 275. According to Klaus Wagenbach, Kafka was attracted to the austere socialism of these Jewish colonies, which were founded on a simple and natural lifestyle. In a novella, the French writer Alain Brossat imagines, with humor and finesse, what Kafka's life as an agricultural laborer in a kibbutz of Hashomer Hatzaïr in Palestine might have been like. See Alain Brossat, *Tête de loir: Kafka in Palestine* (Grenoble: Cent Pages, 1988), 79–112.

55. Jean-Marc Izrine, "Libertaires en Israël," *Débattre* (Spring 2003), 9–10. According to the historian Yaacov Oved, the Hapoel Hatzaïr ("Young Workers') movement, linked with the kibbutzim, was interested in the 1920s in libertarian socialist thinking: their periodical *Ma'abarot* published in 1921 in Hebrew an article of Kropotkin entitled "Anarchic Communism," as well as an essay on Kropotkin's doctrines by the party's principal theoreti-

cian, Chaim Arlozorov. The other movement that was linked to Palestinian collectivist agricultural experiences, Hashomer Hatzaïr ("The Young Guard"), was also, at this time, influenced by the ideas of Landauer and Kropotkin. See Yaacov Oved, "L'anarchismo del Movimento dei Kibbutz," in Amedio Bartolo, ed., *L'Anarchico e l'ebreo: Storia di un incontro* (Milan: Eleuthera, 2001), 202–7.

56. Kafka, *Wedding Preparations*, 119; see Binder, *Kafka Handbuch*, 506–7; and André Breton, "Ce grain de merveilles dans l'aventure," in *Oeuvres complètes*, vol. 3 (Paris: Gallimard, "La Pléiade," 1999), 984. See also Joseph Vogl, *Ort der Gewalt: Kafkas literarische Ethik* (Munich: Wilhelm Fink Verlag, 1990), 198–200, and Glišović, *Politik im Werk Kafkas*, 37–43. After showing that Kafka's proposal is inspired by Tolstoy's anarchism, Glišović describes it as a model for "future kibbutzim." In fact, in this period, kibbutzim had already existed for a decade, and Kafka was certainly aware of them.

57. Franz Kafka, *Letters to Felice*, ed. Erich Heller and Jürgen Born, trans. James Stern and Elizabeth Duckworth (New York: Schocken, 1973), 524–25.

58. André Breton, *Anthologie de l'humour noir* (Paris: Editions du Sagittaire, 1950), 264.

59. Franz Kafka, *Sieben Prosastücke: Ausgewählt und interpretiert von Franz Baumer* (Munich: Kösel Verlag, 1965), 92. See also the illuminating commentary by Bill Dodd: "His texts are not unreflecting expressions of disorientation and despair, but finely observed critiques of power which are presented in an understated, yet provocative manner which in principle affords the reader the possibility of critical orientation. The unobtrusiveness of Kafka's method should not blind us to its ultimately provocative intent." See Bill Dodd, "The Case for a Political Reading," in Julian Preece, ed., *The Cambridge Companion to Kafka* (Cambridge: Cambridge University Press, 2002), 136.

60. André Breton, "Paratonnerre," introduction to *Anthologie de l'humour noir*, 11.

61. Theodor Adorno, "Notes on Kafka" in *Prisms*, trans. Samuel Weber and Shierry Weber (London: Neville Spearman, 1967), 261 [the translation has been slightly changed].

62. I am borrowing the terms "infernal" and "redemption" from Adorno's essay.

63. Rosemarie Ferenczi also uses the term "extreme" to define the utopia of the author of *The Trial*: "Kafka demands a world that is totally just, in the name of all those who suffer injustice; and he says no to the world as he describes it. No doubt he was skeptical about the possibility of realizing this

extreme demand. But he nonetheless proposes it as the goal that must be envisaged." See *Kafka: subjectivité, histoire et structure* (Paris: Klincksieck, 1975), 206.

Chapter 2

1. Elias Canetti, *Kafka's Other Trial*, trans. Christopher Middleton (New York: Schocken, 1974), 80. See also page 87: "Since he fears power in any form, since the real aim of his life is to withdraw from it, in whatever form it may appear, he detects it, identifies it, names it, and creates figures of it in every stance where others would accept it as being nothing out of the ordinary." In an admirable synthesis, Claude David writes at the ending of his preface to the French Pléiade edition of Kafka: "If there is a central idea in Kafka's thinking, it is that of power; the world is organized around power relations; a whole hierarchy is set up that goes from the emperor of China to the lugubrious proprietor of the Castle. At the same time, the most immediate, the best known . . . is the power of the father; the first rung on the ladder of this society of the powerful." See Claude David, "La Fortune de Kafka," in *Oeuvres complètes* (Paris: Gallimard, "La Pléiade," 1976), xvi–xvii.

2. Theodor Adorno, "Notes on Kafka" in *Prisms*, trans. Samuel and Sherry Weber (London: Neville Spearman, 1967), 256. Adorno is probably referencing a passage from Walter Benjamin's essay on Kafka: "The fathers in Kafka's strange families batten on their sons, lying on top of them like giant parasites." Walter Benjamin, "Franz Kafka," in Walter Benjamin, *Selected Writings*, vol. 2, 1927–1934, 796. Benjamin is no doubt thinking of a passage in Kafka's *Letter to His Father*: "vermin, who sting and suck the blood of their victims . . . that is you." Franz Kafka, *Letter to My* Father, trans. Howard Colyer (Lulu: North Carolina, 2008), 81. Benjamin is working under a misunderstanding here: this remark is not directed to the father, but is part of a speech that Kafka attributes to his father, in which he treats his son Franz as a parasite. Admittedly, the rhetorical structure of this section of the *Letter to His Father* is so strange that it's easy to make a mistake . . .

3. Franz Kafka, "Letter to My Father," trans. Howard Colyer (Raleigh, N.C.: Lulu, 2008), 34. According to Ritchie Robertson, Kafka was certainly sympathetic to Zionism in the last seven or eight years of his life, but "his attitude was much more complex, qualified, and individualistic than the one ascribed to him by Brod and Weltsch." See Ritchie Robertson, *Kafka, Judaism, Politics and Literature* (Oxford: Clarendon Press, 1985), 13. To illustrate this complexity, let us remember that according to Hartmut Binder, Kafka

became interested in Zionism between 1915 and 1918, but that "one cannot qualify Kafka's attitude during these last years of his life as Zionist in the generally accepted usage of the word;" it reflects, rather, a sensibility of rejecting assimilation and embracing a diasporic Jewish nationhood. See Hartmut Binder, *Kafka-Handbuch*, vol. 1 (Stuttgart: Kröner, 1979), 572–73. As for Scott Spector, he thinks that it is problematic even to speak of Kafka's "sympathy" for Zionism: according to him, Kafka's relation to Palestine is a narrative construction devoid of any political engagement. See Scott Spector, *Prague Territories. National Conflict and Cultural Innovation in Franz Kafka's Fin de siècle* (Berkeley: Univ. of California Press, 2000), 143. This note is already too long: a detailed discussion of Kafka's relation to Zionism goes beyond the purview of my investigation.

4. Ibid., 44.

5. Ibid., 16.

6. Ibid., 21.

7. Ibid., 76–77.

8. Ibid., 57. [*Translator's note*: In the same passage, Kafka describes his writing as "an intentionally long farewell" from his father.]

9. Kafka, *Diaries, 1910–1913*, 125. See also "Letter to My Father," 14.

10. Franz Kafka, *The Diaries of Franz Kafka, 1914–1923*, trans. Joseph Kresh (New York: Schocken, 1949), 200.

11. One of the paroxysms of this conflict takes place in 1912, when Hermann tries to force Franz to take over, for several weeks, the management of the family factory. A March 8 entry in the *Diaries* reveals the son's despair, who thinks of hurling himself from a window. See Kafka, *Diaries, 1910–1913*, 248.

12. Adorno, *Prisms*, 256; Kafka, "Letter to My Father," 12.

13. Kafka, "Letter to My Father," 35–36.

14. Canetti, *Kafka's Other Trial*, 83. According to Rosemarie Ferenczi, the phrase on siding with 'the workers party" should be taken literally as the statement of a fundamental principle for Kafka, or a central, fixed and unchangeable point of his thought." Rosemarie Ferenczi, *Kafka: subjectivite, histoire et structures*, 22.

15. Kafka, *Diaries, 1910–1913*, 231 [the translation has been slightly changed].

16. Kafka, *Diaries, 1914–1923*, 74–75.

17. Franz Kafka, "Umgang der Versicherungspflicht der Baugewerbe und der baulichen Nebengewerbe," in *Amtliche Schriften*, ed. K. Hermsdorf (Frankfurt am Main: Luchterhand, 1991), 119.

18. Kafka, *Briefe, April 1914–1917*, 364: "If there has been a journal that has attracted me for quite some time . . . it is Dr. Gross's." See also Giuliano Baioni, *Kafka: Letteratura ed Ebraismo* (Turin: Einaudi, 1979), 203–5. On Otto Gross, see Arthur Mitzman, "Anarchism, Expressionism, and Psychoanalysis," *New German Critique* 10, no. 1 (Winter 1977), 77–104. On Hans Gross, see Klaus Wagenbach in Franz Kafka, *In der Strafkolonie: Eine Geschichte aus dem Jahre 1914. Mit Quellen, Chronik und Anmerkungen*, ed. Klaus Wagenbach (Berlin: Verlag Klaus Wagenbach, 1996), 70–71.

19. Franz Kafka, "The Judgment," trans. Willa Muir and Edwin Muir, in Nahum N. Glatzer, ed., *The Complete Stories* (New York: Schocken, 1971), 77–88.

20. See, for example, Karlheinz Fingerhut, "Die Phase des Durchbruchs," in Binder, *Kafka-Handbuch*, 280–82. With similar reasoning, certain commentators find resemblances between "The Judgment" and a play from the Yiddish repertory by Jakob Gordin that Kafka saw: *Got, Mensch und Teufel* (*God, Man, and the Devil*). See Evelyn Torton Beck, "First Impact of the Yiddish Theater: 'The Judgment' (1912)," in *Kafka and the Yiddish Theater* (Madison: University of Wisconsin Press, 1971), 70–121; and Robertson, *Kafka, Judaism*, 35. I am rather struck by the differences between these two works: in Gordin, the hero Herschele is guilty of great infamy: accused by his friend Khatskel, whom he had ruined, he is overcome with guilt and hangs himself. But in "The Judgment," George is perfectly innocent—the accusations of the father are completely unfounded—and the paternal verdict appears as a monstrous injustice.

21. Walter Benjamin, "Franz Kafka," in *Selected Writings*, 2:796.

22. Milan Kundera, "Quelque part là-derrière," *Le Débat* 8 (June 1981), 58.

23. Kafka, *Letters to Felice*. In the same letter he adds: "I meant to describe a war . . . but then the whole thing turned in my hands into something else," 265.

24. Franz Kafka, "The Metamorphosis," in *The Complete Stories*, 122.

25. Ibid., 138.

26. Kafka, "Letter to My Father," 14 and 81. See also the bilingual edition, *Letter to His Father*, trans. Ernst Kaiser and Eithne Wilkins (New York: Schocken, 1976), 122–23.

27. Franz Kafka, *The Man Who Disappeared (America)*, 118.

28. Ibid., 121 and 132–34.

29. The Statue of Liberty was unveiled shortly after the execution of the Chicago anarchists in 1886. Commenting on this coincidence, Kropotkin

denounced the spectacular New York harbor monument as "the statue of the
Goddess of Assassinations." It's not possible to know whether or not Kafka
knew about this remarkable image of the anarchist Russian prince.

30. Kafka, *The Man Who Disappeared (America)*, 141. The head cook, a
maternal figure, is the exception.

31. Ibid., 131; and "Letter to His Father," in *Wedding Preparations*, 181.

32. See Uwe Jahnke, *Die Erfahrung und Entfremdung: Sozialgeschichtliche
Studien zum Werk Franz Kafkas* (Stuttgart: Akademischer Verlag, 1988). He
provides interesting information but exaggerates somewhat the influence of
these Marxist writings on the author.

33. Kafka, *The Man Who Disappeared (America)*, 35. On the affinities between Kafka and the romantic anticapitalism of the Bar-Kochba cercle, see
Ritchie Robertson's above mentioned excellent book *Kafka, Judaism, Politics
and Literature*, 143–55.

34. Ibid., 38.

35. Wilhelm Emrich, *Franz Kafka* (Frankfurt am Main: Athenäum Verlag, 1961), 227–28.

36. Klaus Hermsdorf, *Kafka, Weltbild und Roman* (Berlin: Rutten & Loe-
ning, 1961), 52. According to Dušan Glišović, the novel's "grotesque" presentation of North American capitalism is evidence of Kafka's "prosocialist"
position. See Glišović, *Politik im Werk Kafkas*, 143.

37. Holitscher, *Amerika heute und morgen*, 316. He complains about the
metallic racket of the Chicago factories, a sound that he describes as "cold
and disconsolate like all this modern world, along with its civilization, the
most sinister (*grimmigsten*) enemy of the human race" (321).

38. Ibid., 102–3.

39. Klaus Hermsdorf, "Arbeit und Amt als Erfahrung und Gestaltung," in
Kafka, *Amtliche Schriften*, 33.

40. Brod, *Franz Kafka: A Biography*, 82.

41. Kafka, *Letters to Felice*, 149. See also *Briefe an Felice und andere Kor-
respondez aus der Verlobungszeit* (Frankfurt am Main: S. Fischer Verlag,
1970), 241. Kafka seems to make an intimate association between capitalism
and the catastrophe of a total mechanization. Here is what Janouch reports
him as saying during a conversation: "The factories are merely organizations
for increasing financial profit. In such a matter, we all have merely a subor-
dinate function. Man is today only an old-fashioned instrument of economic growth, a hangover from history, whose economically inadequate
skills will soon be displaced by frictionless thinking machines." Janouch,
Conversations with Kafka, 103.

42. Ibid., 115.

43. Kafka, *Diaries, 1914–1923*, 188.

44. Kafka, *The Man Who Disappeared (America)*, 15.

45. Adorno, *Prisms*, 246 [the translation has been slightly changed].

46. Kurt Tucholsky, "In der Stafkolonie," *Gesammelte Werke*, vol. 1 (Hamburg: Rowohlt, 1960), 644–55. Arguing against Tucholsky, Dušan Glišović claims that this novella is not about power: according to him the officer is merely a representative of Kafka himself, and the steel needle that pierces the head at the end of the narrative is the pen with which the writer composes his works! I have trouble taking this bizarre and apolitical interpretation seriously, which is paradoxically proposed in the book titled *Politics in Kafka's Oeuvre*. See Glišović, *Politik im Werk Kafkas*, 95–104.

47. Enzo Traverso, *L'Histoire déchirée: Essai sur Auschwitz et les intellectuels* (Paris: Cerf, 1997), 52–53.

48. Sander Gilman draws some interesting parallels between the situation of Dreyfus on Devil's Island—the fact that he was chained to his bed—and the themes of Kafka's novella, but in the final analysis the victim of "In the Penal Colony" is not a French Jewish captain but an anonymous indigenous man; Gilman's analysis is not convincing. See Sander Gilman, *Franz Kafka: The Jewish Patient* (London: Routledge, 1995), 69–87.

49. There is an excellent study about Kafka's possible sources in (mostly German) writings on penal colonies: Walter Muller-Seidel, *Die Deportation des Menschen* (Stuttgart: Metzler, 1986). However, the author does not dispute the fact that there are no deported persons in the novella.

50. See Edward Said, *Culture and Imperialism* (London: Vintage, 1994). For a systematic presentation of the works or events that could have inspired this novella by Kafka, see the remarkable edition by Klaus Wagenbach. According to the critic Paul Peters, the title of the novella is meant to suggest that colonialism itself is based on the oppression and punishing of the colonials. See Paul Peters, "Witness to the Execution: Kafka and Colonialism," *Monatshefte* 93, no. 4 (2001), 402.

51. Roy Pascal convincingly criticizes the false apologetic "religious" readings of the novella—readings that celebrate the "redemption" of the man sentenced to death by torture. See Roy Pascal, *Kafka's Narrators: A Study of His Stories and Sketches* (Cambridge: Cambridge University Press, 1982), 78–80. See also Herbert Kraft, *Mondheimat: Kafka* (Pfullingen: Verlag Neske, 1983), 109–13, and Paul Peters, who demonstrates the absurdity of the interpretation that compares the old commandant with Moses (as Ingeborg Henel does) or with Yahweh (as Erwin R. Steinberg does), as if Jew-

ish law were not founded on the categorical refusal of any human sacrifice.
See Peters, "Witness to the Execution," 422.

52. In reading these lines that conclude the novella, one can't help thinking of the policies of the old European colonial powers during the past decades, which try at all costs to prevent the former colonized subjects from
coming to the European continent.

53. Franz Kafka, "In the Penal Colony," in *The Complete Stories*, 140–44.

54. Kafka, *Diaries, 1914–1923*, 246.

55. A commentary cited by Janouch confirms Kafka's antimilitarism: the
military system suppresses the individual and transforms free persons into
"an organized unit in a group, which obeys a word of command that is fun-
damentally alien to them. In that way they are the ideal of all commanding
officers. Nothing has to be explained, nothing improvised. The word of command is enough . . . the soldier(s) . . . parade like puppets." As an example
Kafka cites Italian fascism! See Janouch, *Conversations with Kafka*, 129.

56. Kafka, *Wedding Preparations*, 231. The text is undated, but is found
near another one dated August 20, 1916; one can suppose that it was composed during the war. Admittedly, Kafka once considered enlisting, but this
was the result of a desperate attempt to extricate himself from a difficult
personal situation (his engagement with Felice Bauer), rather than a desire
to join the military.

57. Kafka, "In the Penal Colony," 147.

58. Ibid., 149.

59. One of the concerns of the Prague anarchists was precisely the reification of individuals in the military system: "Militarism is one of the most violent things that the state imposes on the liberty of individuals . . . the soldier
is an individual, a male human who is forced, in certain situations, to play
the role of a thing." This comes from a 1905 article by the Czech anarchist
Frana Sramek, quoted in Tomek, *Volk!* 27.

60. Kafka, *Letters to Felice*, 531 and appendix, 580. See *Briefe an Felice*,
764–66 (the text of Kafka's speech is included in a letter of October 30,
1916).

61. Janouch, *Conversations with Kafka*, 19.

62. Manfred Frank and G. Kurz, eds., *Materialien zu Schellings philoso-
phische Anfängen* (Frankfurt am Main: Suhrkamp, 1975), 110.

63. Astride Lange-Kirchheim has interestingly drawn a parallel between
the article by Alfred Weber and Kafka's novella. However, her attempt to find
systematic analogies between them, sentence by sentence and word for
word—which suggests that the novella is entirely constructed on the basis of

the sociological essay—seems, finally, unconvincing. She ends up with absurd claims, such as suggesting that there is a parallelism between Weber's description of the higher and lower levels of bureaucracy and the higher and lower structures of the killing machine described by the Prague author. See Astride Lange-Kirchheim, "Alfred Weber und Franz Kafka," in Eberhard Daemm, ed., *Alfred Weber als Politiker und Gelehrter* (Stuttgart: Franz Steiner Verlag, 1986), 113–49.

64. Karel Kosik, "Hasek et Kafka ou le monde du grotesque," *Lettre internationale* 1 (1964), 66; Adorno, *Prisms*, 260. Finally, even an "official" author of the GDR like Klaus Hermsdorf—who accuses the author of *The Trial* of "petit-bourgeois subjectivism"—admits that no other writer so insightfully perceived bureaucracy (as an impersonal system that becomes autonomous and that transforms itself into an alienating apparatus, as an end in itself) as the great power of the era and as a lethal menace to humanity. See Hermsdorf, *Kafka: Weltbild und Roman*, 85.

Chapter 3

1. Hannah Arendt, *The Jew as Pariah: Jewish Identity and Politics in the Modern Age* (New York: Grove Press, 1978), 84.

2. Ibid., 87.

3. Franz Kafka, "The Eight Octavo Notebooks," in *Wedding Preparations*, 114. A longer discussion of Kakfa's relation to Zionism is beyond the scope of this essay.

4. This interest is documented in several passages of his letters edited by Max Brod, *Briefe, 1902–1924*. His concerns about anti-Semitism in Prague and his desire to leave are also expressed in his *Letters to Milena*, 50–51 and 196.

5. Hannah Arendt, "Franz Kafka," in *Sechs Essays* (Heidelberg: Lambert Schneider, 1948), 130–45. This is the expanded and edited German version of the essay published earlier in the *Partisan Review*.

6. There is also a third school of interpretation, according to which *The Trial* would be an autobiographical novel in which political questions play only a marginal or secondary role. Without a doubt the novel was written at the moment of the author's breaking off his engagement with Felice Bauer, whose initials, F. B., appear as Fräulein Bürstner in the book. It's also true that Kafka described his meeting with Felice and her family at the Askanier Hof hotel in Berlin as a sort of trial: "I realized that . . . I could save the situation by making some startling confession." Kafka, *Letters to Felice*, 437. He

also refers to her in a letter dated September 30 or October 1, 1917, as his "human tribunal" (*Letters to Felice*, 545). To go from that to making the novel a sort of allegory of Kafka's "guilt" about the failure of his engagement is only a short step, and one that many have happily taken. They forget that in the novel, the meeting of Joseph K. with F. B.—a long conversation and a stolen kiss—takes place after his arrest and indictment. Dušan Glišović pushes this type of reading to its extreme limit in suggesting that the knife that executes Joseph K. is a symbol of the writer's pen, the pen that kept him twice from marrying Felice Bauer. See Glišović, *Politik im Werk Kafkas*, 151–52. Once again, the critic ignores the text as it is actually written and attributes "symbolic" or allegorical meanings to different episodes in the novel.

7. Arendt, "Franz Kafka," in *Six Essays*, 130.

8. Erich Heller, *Kafka* (London: William Collins Sons, 1974), 88.

9. Casten Schlingmann, *Franz Kafka* (Stuttgart: Reclam, 1995), 44.

10. Kafka, *The Trial*, trans. Mike Mitchell (New York: Oxford University Press, 2009), 5 [the translation has been slightly changed].

11. In expressing his innocence throughout the novel, Joseph K. is not lying, but expressing his heartfelt conviction. It's the reason why, at the moment the policemen announce his imprisonment, he thinks it's a practical joke organized by his office mates. This is the reaction of someone with a — clear conscience! To be sure, in the *Diaries*, Kafka calls Joseph K. "guilty" as opposed to the innocent Karl Rossmann—even if both are condemned to death. But the question remains: guilty in whose eyes? In those of the author or of the tribunal that condemns him without giving him the chance to defend himself? The second alternative is the only one that corresponds to the spirit and the letter of the novel.

12. Arendt, *Sechs Essays*, 128.

13. Bertolt Brecht, "Sur la literature tchécosolovaque moderne," in *Le Siè-cle de Kafka*, ed. Avenarius Nemcová et al. (Paris: Centre Georges Pompidou, 1984), 162. In an essay published in 1974, J. P. Stern suggests an interesting (through perhaps a bit forced) parallel between Kafka's *Trial* and the Nazi laws or the actions of the tribunals of the Third Reich. J. P. Stern, "The Law of the Trial," in Franz Kuna, ed., *On Kafka: Semi-centenary Perspectives* (New York: Harper & Row, 1976).

14. [*Translator's note*: The "Moscow Trials" refers to the trials of the old Bolshevik leaders by Stalin.]

15. Walter Benjamin, "Notes from Svendborg, Summer 1934," in *Selected Writings*, 2:785 and 787. According to Brecht, the perspective of Kafka is

"that of a man who has fallen under the wheels" of power.(quoted in Benjamin, 787).

16. Kafka, *The Trial*, 7.

17. I am basing myself here on Ferenczi, *Kafka*. See page 62: "Kafka did not wish to be the prophet of future catastrophes; he limited himself to deciphering aspects of the tragedies of his times. If his descriptions seem prophetic, it's only because the later eras are the logical outcome of Kafka's own."

18. Kafka, *Letters to Felice* (October 28, 1916), 530. See the chapter "Kafka Wept" in Gilman, *Franz Kafka: The Jewish Patient*.

19. Kafka, *Briefe, 1902–1924*, 402. Sander Gilman thinks that the Dreyfus affair haunted Kafka during the whole of his adult life and that it furnished the model for *The Trial*, but he doesn't provide any documentary evidence for this statement. See Gilman, *Franz Kafka: The Jewish Patient*, 69–70.

20. Janouch, *Kafka und seine Welt*, 55. On the Hilsner affair and its impact on Czech opinion, see Ferenczi, *Kafka*, 46–58.

21. Kafka, *Briefe, 1918–1920*, 189.

22. Max Brod, *Franz Kafka: Eine Biographie (Erinnerungen und Dokumente)* (Frankfurt am Main: S. Fischer, 1954), 248. Brod cites Dora Dymant, Kafka's last companion: "According to Dora, among the burned papers there was a tale that Kafka wrote about the trial in Kiev of Beiliss for the crime of ritual murder." See Arnold J. Band, "Kafka and the Beiliss Affair," *Comparative Literature* 32, no. 2 (Spring 1980), 168–83.

23. According to Rosemarie Ferenczi, the manipulation of the Hilsner affair by the state taught Kafka, even beyond the limits of Jewish reality, how far "unscrupulous power could go." Ferenczi, *Kafka*, 61. See also her comment, page 205: "*The Trial* is an indictment against an era in which something like the Hilsner affair was possible."

24. Hannah Arendt, Karl Jaspers, "Letter of March 4, 1951," *Correspondance 1926–1969* (Paris: Payot, 1985), 244.

25. Eleni Varikas, "Le Fardeau de notre temps: Parias et critique de la modernité politique chez Arendt," in Marie Claire Caloz-Tschopp, ed., *Hannah Arendt, les sans-État et le "droit d'avoir des droits"* (Paris: Flammarion, 1998), 73.

26. Kafka, "Fragments from Note-Books and Loose Pages," in *Wedding Preparations*, 365–66.

27. Kafka, *The Trial*, 105.

28. Ibid., 32.

29. Ibid., 110.

30. Ibid., 50.

31. Ibid., 77.

32. Ibid., 85–86.

33. Ibid., 139.

34. Ibid., 162.

35. Ibid., 165.

36. Etienne de la Boétie, *The Politics of Obedience: The Discourse of Voluntary Servitude*, trans. Harry Kurz (Montreal: Black Rose Books, 1997).

37. Ibid., 163.

38. Arendt, "Franz Kafka," 4.

39. Franz Kafka, *Tagebücher 1910–1923* (New York: Schocken, 1949), 420–21.

40. A few months after writing this conclusion, I came across this wonderful statement by the Austrian nonconformist Peter Handke: "Since the beginning of writing there has been no better text to help the oppressed resist with dignity while at the same time remaining indignant toward the order of the world than the end of the novel *The Trial*, where Joseph K., the hero, is dragged to slaughter and himself accelerates his own execution." Peter Handke, "Discours de reception du prix Kafka," in Nemcová et al., *Le Siècle de Kafka*, 248.

Chapter 4

1. Franz Kafka, "Letter to Grete Bloch, June 11, 1914," in *Letters to Felice*, 423. See also the letter to Felice from September 16, 1916: "I wouldn't think of going to the synagogue. . . . One can do this today no more than one could as a child; I still remember how as a boy I almost suffocated from the terrible boredom and pointlessness of the hours in the synagogue." *Letters to Felice*, 502.

2. Kafka, "The Eight Octavo Notebooks," 43 and 88 [I have slightly amended the translation].

3. Charles Taylor, *A Secular Age*, Cambridge, Harvard University Press, 2007, 302.

4. Ibid., 73.

5. Max Brod, "Verzweiflung und Erlösung im Werk Franz Kafkas," in *Über Franz Kafka*, 213. According to Brod, it is not Kafka's novels that contain expressions of faith in divine promise and redemption but his aphorisms. However, his argument is far from being convincing.

6. Gershom Scholem, *Walter Benjamin und sein Engel* (Frankfurt am Main: Suhrkamp, 1983), 32–33. Commenting on Scholem's text, Stéphane

Mosès tellingly writes: "If we are to call this interpretation theological, it can only be in the sense of a negative theology by which all we can say about God is the very fact of his absence." See Stéphane Mosès, *L'Ange de l'histoire: Rosenzweig, Benjamin, Scholem* (Paris: Seuil, 1992), 208.

7. Adorno, *Prisms*, 252.

8. Kafka, *The Trial*, 165.

9. I attempted to analyze this "elective affinity" in the chapter on Kafka in my book *Redemption and Utopia: Jewish Libertarian Thought in Central Europe. An Elective Affinity*, trans. Hope Heaney (London: Athlone Press, 1992).

10. Wagenbach, *Kafka in Selbstzeugnissen*, 98.

11. Kafka, *The Trial*, 155.

12. I'm following here an argument by Jeffrey Veidlinger, *The Moscow State Yiddish Theater. Jewish Culture on the Soviet Stage*, Bloominmgton: Indiana University Press, 2000, 14. The examples mentioned are, among others, Franz Kafka, Sigmund Freud, and Phillip Roth.

13. Kafka, *The Trial*, 159 [the translation has been slightly changed].

14. Jacques Derrida, "Préjugés," in *La Faculté de juger* (Paris: Ed. De Minuit, 1985), 113.

15. Ibid., 128.

16. Brod, *Franz Kafka: Eine Biographie*, 215.

17. Hartmut Binder, "Vor dem Gesetz," in *Einführung in Kafka's Welt* (Stuttgart: J. B. Metzler, 1993), 222–24 and 246.

18. Baioni, *Kafka: Letteratura ed Ebraismo*, n.p.

19. Scott Spector, "Kafka und die literarische Moderne" in *Kafka Handbuch. Leben, Werk, Wirkung*, eds. Oliver Jahraus and Bettina von Jagow, Gottingen, Vandenhoek & Ruprecht, 2008, 191.

20. Hugo Bergmann, "Die Heiligung des Names (Kiddush Hashem)," *Vom Judentum: Ein Sammelbuch* (Prague: Verein Jüdischer Hochschüler Bar Kochba, 1913), 40–41.

21. Hugo Bergmann, "Pesach und die Menschen unserer Zeit," *Jawne und Jerusalem* (Berlin: Jüdischer Verlag, 1919), 78–79.

22. Kafka, *Diaries, 1910–1913*, 324.

23. Commenting on this formulation, Rosemarie Ferenczi writes: "It's in this precise place, the crossing of the paths of liberty and slavery, that he sees the world—and describes it in his novels." Ferenczi, *Kafka*, 48.

24. Felix Wetsch, *Gnade und Freiheit* (Munich: K. Wolff, 1920), 37 and 73; see also Marina Cavarocchi, *La certeza che toglie la speranza: Contributo per l'approfondimento dell'aspetto ebraico in Kafka* (Florence: Giuntina,

1988), 92–99. These topics were present in the conversations and correspondence between Franz Kafka and Felix Weltsch long before the book's publication. When he received the manuscript in 1919, Kafka sent his friend a list of corrections and commentaries. See Harmut Binder, "Ein ungedrucktes Schreiben Franz Kafkas an Felix Weltsch," *Jahrbuch der deutschen Schillergesellschaft* 20 (1976), 109–30. In a letter to Felix Weltsch in the spring of 1920, Kafka recognized that this book was "highly important" for him.

25. Kafka, *Diaries, 1910–1913*, 323.

26. Kafka, *Briefe 1902–1924*, 279.

27. Kafka, *Diaries, 1914–1923*, 92.

28. Felix Weltsch, "Freiheit und Schuld in Franz Kafka's Roman 'Der Prozess,'" *Jüdischer Almanch aus dem Jahr 5687* (1926–27), 115–21.

29. Walter H. Sokel, *Franz Kafka: Tragik und Ironie* (Munich: Albert Langen, 1964), 215; Ernst Fischer, "Kafka Conference," in Kenneth Hughes, ed., *Franz Kafka: An Anthology of Marxist Criticism* (London: University Press of New England, 1981), 91.

30. Marthe Robert, *Seul comme Franz Kafka* (Paris: Calmann-Lévy, 1979), 162. See also Ingeborg Henel, "The Legend of the Doorkeeper and Its Significance for Kafka's Trial," in James Rolleston, ed., *Twentieth Century Interpretations of "The Trial"* (Englewood Cliffs, NJ: Prentice-Hall, 1976), 41 and 48.

31. Jürgen Born, "Kafkas Türhüterlegende: Versuch einer positiven Deutung," in *Jenseits der Gleichnisse: Kafka und sein Werk* (Bern: Peter Lang, 1986), 177–80. A similar reading is proposed by Leandro Konder: the man's sin is obedience, the opposite of what the Bible ascribes to Adam. Kafka's parable teaches us that "in order to reach real justice . . . one has to resolutely confront the false justice that the illegitimate authorities try to impose on us." The fable is therefore a "call to action." See Leandro Konder, *Kafka* (Rio de Janeiro: J. Alvaro, 1976), 144.

32. Arendt, *Sechs Essays*, 133.

33. Martin Buber, *Die Chassidischen Bücher* (Hellerau: Jakob Hegner, 1929), 40–47.

34. See Moshé Shalev, "It is suicide not to go to the synagogue" (translated from the Hebrew), *Haaretz*, literary supplement "Tarbut V Sifrut," October 15, 1997, 34.

35. Ulf Abraham, "Moses 'Vor dem Gesetz': Eine unbekannte Vorlage zu Kafkas 'Türhüterlegende,'" *Deutsche Vierteljahrsschrift für Literaturwissenschaft und Geistesgeschichte* 57 (1983), 636–41. Other researchers had already claimed that certain Talmudic tales and fables transmitted to Kafka by

his friend Yitzhak Löwy had profoundly influenced such works as *The Trial* and, in particular, the parable *Before the Law*. See Walter Sokel, "Franz Kafka as a Jew," *Leo Baeck Institute Yearbook* 18 (1973), 238. Until now one hadn't found any precise sources to support this hypothesis.

36. Kafka, *Briefe 1902–1924*, 334 [November 1920].

37. Kafka, *Letters to Felice*, September 11, 1916, 499. See also the letter to Felice from May 6, 1915: "This life [of Lily Braun] really is worth sharing. How it longs to sacrifice itself, and does! A veritable suicide and a resurrection while still alive." *Letters to Felice*, 454.

38. Lily Braun, *Memorien einer Sozialistin* (1909; Berlin: J.H.W. Dietz, 1985), 82–83.

39. See also *Letters to Felice*, 486, 498–99, 521.

40. Franz Kafka, "The Problem of Our Laws," in *The Great Wall of China: Stories and Reflections*, trans. Willa Muir and Edwin Muir (New York: Schocken, 1970), 149.

41. Kafka, *Diaries, 1910–1913*, 307.

42. Franz Kafka, *Tagebücher 1909–1923* (Frankfurt am Main: S. Fischer, 1997), 557 (*Eindringen kann ich scheinbar in die Welt nicht, aber ruhig liegen, empfangen, das Empfangene in mir ausbreiten und dann ruhig vertreten.*) Of course, these passages are not unambiguous and could be read in several different ways. For example, the one from 1913 ends with an expression of doubt: "Only I don't know whether I want this."

43. Kafka, "The Eight Octavo Note-Books," 86.

44. Ibid., 88.

45. Martin Buber, *Judaïsme*, trans. Marie-José Jolivet (Lagrasse: Verdier, 1982), 29; and *Die Chassidischen Bücher* (Berlin: Schocken, 1927), xxiii–xxvii. See also Martin Buber, "Jewish Religiosity," in *On Judaism* (New York: Schocken, 19667), 79–107.

46. Franz Rosenzweig, *Star of Redemption*, trans. Barbara E. Galli (Madison: University of Wisconsin Press, 2005), 305.

47. Max Weber, *Economy and Society*, ed. Guenther Roth and Claus Wittich, trans. Ephraim Fischoff et al., vol. 1 (Berkeley: University of California Press, 1978), 576–77. See also vol. 2: "Every ethically oriented religiosity begins with eschatological hopes and hence rejects the world" (1187).

Chapter 5

1. Max Brod, "Nachwort," in Franz Kafka, *Das Schloss* (Munich: Kurt Wolff Verlag, 1926), 495–96 and 500–501. Certain commentators who want

despite everything to attribute a religious significance to the behavior of the high officials of the Castle (their lies, deceptions, and concupiscence) end up comparing them to the Greek gods. This is the surprising theory of Pietro Citati, according to whom the officials would be pagan and polytheist gods who, like the Greek gods, "sometimes come among men . . . drawn by a female body." See Pietro Citati, *Kafka* (Paris: Gallimard, 1991), 302–14. To make Kafka into a Hellenizing pagan is not very credible, but it represents the logical conclusion of any attempt to make the Lords of the Castle into gods or divine messengers. It's true that in a dream of K. the official Bürgel appears as a Greek god, but it's "a comical spectacle" in which the secretary is completely nude and finds himself in a difficult position in relation to K. during a struggle: "That Greek god squealed like a girl being tickled." Franz Kafka, *The Castle*, trans. Anthea Bell (Oxford: Oxford University Press, 2009), 231. Thus the pagan references in *The Castle* only appear as comedy.

2. Heller, *Kafka*, 131.

3. Günter Anders, *Kafka: Pro und Contra* (Munich: C.H. Beck, 1963), 88–89. According to Anders, in the face of iniquitous power, Kafka's characters bow down. The behavior of the surveyor K.—the "hero" of the Castle—consists, he says, in conforming to all the regulations, in interiorizing them and even in justifying the "immoral" demands of those in power. Consequently Kafka, as author, is a "moralist of conformity," and his political message is simply to "abase oneself." Anders attributes to K. a servile behavior that does not correspond in any way to what one can read in the novel. As I will show, it's exactly the opposite.

4. [*Translator's note*: Marcion of Sinope was an early leader of Christianity who rejected the God of the Old Testament, whom he regarded as a cruel and despotic demiurge.]

5. Martin Buber, "Zwei Glaubenswesen," in *Werke*, vol. 1 (Heidelberg: Laubert Schneider, 1962), 778. Hans Joachim Schoeps also defines Kafka's religion as a theology of the absence of salvation (*Heillosigkeit*) and adds: "Only Jewish theology knows the phenomenon of an authentic history of nonsalvation (*Unheilsgeschichte*), in which the history of salvation is transformed into its polar opposite." Hans Joachim Schoeps, "Theologische Motive in der Dichtung Franz Kafkas," *Die Neue Rundschau* 62, no. 1 (1951), 21.

6. Kafka, *Wedding Preparations*, 51. [I have slightly amended the translation from the German.]

7. Adorno, *Prisms*, 269. The first to speak of "hell" and "infernal violence" in Kafka—in a 1925 review of *The Trial*—was his friend Ernst Weiss.

See *Franz Kafka: Kritik und Rezeption 1924–1938* (Frankfurt am Main: S. Fischer, 1983), 95–96.

8. Kafka, "Fourth Octavo Notebook," in *Wedding Preparations*, 102–3.

9. György Lukács, *The Theory of the Novel*, trans. Anna Bostock (Cambridge, Mass: MIT Press, 1985), 93.

10. Kafka, *The Castle*, 11.

11. This is Alfred Döblin's position in "Die Romane von Franz Kafka," *Die Literarische Welt*, March 4, 1927.

12. Kafka, *The Castle*, 60.

13. As an informed reader of Kafka observes: "The purpose of the protocol is the protocol, the purpose of order is order, the purpose of administration is administration and so on in an infinite circle. Everything ends and freezes in repetition." Karin Keller, *Gesellschaft in mythischem Bann: Studien zum Roman "Das Schloss" und anderen Werken Franz Kafkas* (Wiesbaden: Akademische Verlagsgesellschaft Athenaion, 1977), 62.

14. Kafka, *The Castle*, 63.

15. See the interesting analyses of Axel Dornemann, *Im Labyrinth der Bürokratie: Tolstojs "Auferstehung" und Kafkas "Schloss"* (Heidelberg: Carl Winter Unversitätsverlag, 1984), 109.

16. As Leandro Konder observes, Kafka's humor consists in the demythification of "rationalist" discourse that is used to excuse irrational behavior. See Leandro Konder, *Franz Kafka* (Rio de Janeiro: J. Alvaro, 1967), 122.

17. José Maria Gonzalez Garciá, *La maquina bureaucratica: Afinidades electivas entre Max Weber y Kafka* (Madrid: Visor, 1989), 42–43 and 161–67. On the same subject, see the illuminating comments by Enzo Traverso, *L'Histoire déchirée op.cit.*, 45–57.

18. Max Weber, *Gesammelte Aufsätze zur Soziologie und Sozialpolitik* (Tübingen: Mohr, 1924), 412.

19. Alfred Weber, "Der Beamte," *Neue Rundschau* (October 1910), 1321–22, 1329, 1333. Interestingly, Weber writes that Jews are exempt from this servitude because they are rejected and excluded by the bureaucratic apparatus, which forces them into a more subjective individual existence. This makes one think of the land surveyor K. Lange-Kirchheim has suggested some correspondences between the sociologist's article and some themes of *The Castle*. See Lange-Kirchheim, "Alfred Weber und Franz Kafka."

20. Kafka, *The Castle*, 229.

21. Ibid., 173.

22. See Malcolm Paisley, *Das Schloss* (Frankfurt: S. Fischer, 1994), 240.

23. Kafka, *The Castle*, 238.

24. Ibid., 103 [the translation has been slightly changed].

25. Ibid., 186.

26. Adorno, "Notes on Kafka," 256. The episode with Amalia could be the starting point for a fascinating feminist study of *The Castle*. There is in fact a text that calls itself "a feminist approach to *The Castle*," but it is very disappointing: according to the author, Sortini, far from being a villain, is simply "an ageing, incompetent letter-writer in love with a maiden," a "wooer inviting Amalia up to his castle." See Elisabeth Boas, "Feminist Approaches: The Castle," in *Kafka: Gender, Class, and Race in the Letters and Fictions* (Oxford: Clarendon Press, 1996), 251, 261. Does this need further comment?

27. The libertarian socialist Gustav Landauer had translated Étienne de la Boétie's *De la servitude volontaire* into German and published it in his journal *Der Sozialist* in 1910 and 1911. We don't know whether Kafka knew this work, but it's likely that the Prague anarchists with whom he associated knew it.

28. Canetti, *Kafka's Other Trial*, 83.

29. Kafka, "Fragments from Note-Books and Loose Pages," 320–21.

30. Franz Kafka, "The Refusal," trans. Tania Stern and James Stern, in *The Complete Stories*, 265–67. According to Janouch, in Kafka's eyes voluntary servitude was the general rule in modern society: "Every man lives behind bars, which he carries within him. . . . Safe in the shelter of the herd, they march through the streets of the cities, to their work, to their feeding troughs, to their pleasures. . . . There are no longer any marvels, only regulations, prescriptions, directives. Men are afraid of freedom and responsibility. So they prefer to hide behind the prison bars which they build around themselves." See Janouch, *Conversations with Kafka*, 22–23.

31. Kafka, *The Castle*, 161. See also K.'s exclamation: "What strange folk you are!" (182). Yet this K. is in no way a revolutionary. After the passage quoted above, he goes on to say: "If authorities are good authorities, why shouldn't people go in awe of them?" But this conditional "if" introduces an element of doubt: is this Castle administration really so good?

32. Kafka, *The Castle*, 46.

33. Zygmunt Bauman, "Strangers, the Social Construction of Universality and Particularity," *Telos* 78 (Winter 1988–89), 31–32. In the second version of her article for *Partisan Review*, Hannah Arendt writes: "The outstanding characteristic of the K. in *The Castle* is that he is interested only in universals, in those things to which all men have a natural right." Arendt, "Franz Kafka: A Reevaluation," 415.

34. Kafka, *The Castle*, 6, 9.

35. Ibid., 32

36. Ibid., 81.

37. The passage was crossed out by Kafka but reported by Max Brod in his 1946 afterword to *The Castle*. See Kafka, *Das Schloss*, 428–29.

38. Kafka, *The Castle*, 64.

39. Ibid., 147.

40. Ibid., 49.

41. Ibid., 82. As Hannah Arendt expresses it so well, "he discovers that the normal world and normal society are in fact abnormal, that the universally accepted judgments of the law-abiding (*Wohlanständigen*) are in fact insane, and that the actions that result from following the rules of this game are in fact disastrous for everyone." See Hannah Arendt, "Franz Kafka" (1944) in *Die verborgene Tradition* (Frankfurt am Main, Suhrkamp, 1976), 100.

42. Ibid., 171.

43. Cited by Max Brod in his afterword to the 1946 edition; see Kafka, *Das Schloss*, 429. I have already mentioned K's negative response to the suggestion that he has come to "bring happiness."

44. Kafka, *The Castle*, 108.

45. Ibid., 162.

46. Ibid., 246.

47. Ibid., 196.

48. Marthe Robert, *As Lonely as Franz Kafka*, trans. Karl Mannheim (New York: Schocken, 1982), 175.

49. Hannah Arendt, "Franz Kafka," in *Die verborgene Tradition* 102. [*Translator's note*: see also Arendt, *The Jew as Pariah*, 87–88: "K's idea seems to be that much could be accomplished, if only one simple man could achieve to live his own life like a normal human being."]

50. Kafka, *The Castle*, 254. The critic David Suchoff describes this dream of Pepi's as "anarchist," as an "apocalyptic liberation" by fire of Pepi and her fellow workers from the domination of the *Herren* (gentlemen, masters) they serve. See David Suchoff, *Critical Theory and the Novel. Mass Society and Cultural Criticism in Dickens, Melville, and Kafka* (Madison: University of Wisconsin Press, 1994), 175.

51. Ibid., 169–70.

52. Ibid., 173.

53. Ibid., 170.

54. Ibid., 182. The behavior of her younger brother Barnabas is quite dif-

ferent; as Olga says, he "dares not speak to anyone for fear he might lose his job through some kind of unintentional infringement of unknown rules" (161); "It's hard to understand why, when he was so brave as a boy, he has now so entirely lost his courage as a man up there" (199).

55. The eminent specialist and philologist Bert Nagel makes a serious error when he comments: "In Kafka, women always appear not only as marginal and secondary figures, but also as people of an inferior moral standing. In his entire oeuvre one can hardly find an appealing female figure, or even a honest woman." See Bert Nagel, *Kafka und die Weltliteratur* (Munich: Winkler Verlag, 1983), 237. One wonders whether this critic even read *The Castle*. Kafka's sympathy for courageous and nonconformist women who broke with convention in order to follow the dictates of their conscience is confirmed, among others, by his admiration for and even fascination with Lily Braun, whose works he distributed to his male and female friends. He was equally attracted to Milena Jesenska, whose brave spirit he praises in his letter of June 13, 1920: "My fear . . . keeps increasing, for it signifies a withdrawal from the world, thus increase of its pressure, thus further increase of fear; your courage, on the other hand, signifies a going forward, thus decrease of pressure, thus growth of courage." Kafka, *Letters to Milena*, 58.

56. Kafka, "Letter to My Father," 42–43.

Chapter 6

1. Georg Lukács, *The Meaning of Contemporary Realism*, trans. John Mander and Necke Mander (London: Merlin Press, 1963), 15.

2. Ibid., 76.

3. Ibid., 77–82. The association of Thomas Mann with "health" is all the more outrageous in light of the fact that illness occupies a central place in his major works (*Death in Venice*, *The Magic Mountain*, *Doctor Faustus*).

4. Not without reason, as we shall soon see. The history of the Stalinist reception of Kafka would merit its own chapter (but would lead us too far astray from our subject). It would start from the discussion appearing in 1945 in the French Communist journal *Action* around the question "Should Kafka be burned?" and would continue on to the (more or less) well-intentioned attempts at rehabilitation by Roger Garaudy and others during the 1960s.

5. Lukács, *Meaning of Contemporary Realism*, 26 and 53.

6. There is an interesting Marxist criticism of Lukács's writings on Kafka in Carlos Nelson Coutinho, "Kafka: pressupostos historicos e exposição estética," *Temas de Ciencias Humanas* 2 (1977).

7. I heard this story during a conversation in Budapest with Agnes Heller and Ferenc Feher. It is mentioned in a book by the German essayist Fritz Raddatz, *Lukács* (Hamburg: Rowolt, 1972), 116.

8. György Lukács, "Vorwort," in *Werke*, vol. 6 (Berlin: Luchterhand, 1965), 9. Among the writers who recognize the realism of Kafka, Wilhelm Emerich stands out because of the special place he accords to the Prague writer: "Kafka is the only writer of our century who recognized, in critical fashion, the immanent laws of our social reality. . . . This is why he is the most realistic writer of our era. It is also why he is its most enigmatic poet . . . for everyone who uncritically accepts these immanent laws." Wilhelm Emerich, *Geist und Widergeist: Wahrheit und Lüge der Literatur. Studien* (Frankfurt am Main: Athenäum Verlag, 1965), 300–310.

9. Goldstücker et al, *Franz Kafka aus Prager Sicht*. For a discussion of the impact of this event, see the interesting essay (originally published in a Trotskyist journal) by Alain Brossat, "Kafka miroir de Khrouchtchev," in *Un communisme insupportable* (Paris: L'Harmattan, 1992).

10. Fischer, "Kafka Conference," 85.

11. Ibid., 77.

12. Ibid., 93.

13. Ibid., 85; and Jiri Hajek, "Kafka and the Socialist World," in Hughes, *Anthology of Marxist Criticism*, 122.

14. Fischer, "Kafka Conference," 77.

15. Kafka, *Diaries, 1914–1923*, 110.

16. Breton, "Ce grain de merveilleux," 984. The quotation from Rimbaud comes from a letter to Paul Demeny dated May 15, 1871 (one of the famous "Lettres du Voyant"). Gustav Janouch attributes to Kafka the following comment on Rimbaud, which has a remarkable affinity with statements made by the surrealists about the magic of art: "He transforms vowels into colors. By this wizardry of sound and color he comes near to the magical religious practices of primitive races." Janouch, *Conversations with Kafka*, 186. Breton's admiration for Kafka does not of course mean that he considered the Prague writer to be a "surrealist."

17. Dornemann, *Im Labyrinth der Burokratie*, 204.

18. For instance Gerd-Klaus Kaltenbrunner and Friedhart Hegner, cited by Dornemann, ibid., 36.

19. Lewis A. Coser, ed., *Sociology through Literature* (Englewood Cliffs, N.J.: Prentice Hall, 1972), 233.

20. Marthe Robert, *L'Ancien et le nouveau, de "Don Quichotte" à Kafka* (Paris: Payot, 1967), 195.

Chapter 7

1. George Steiner, *De la Bible à Kafka* (Paris: Bayard, 2002), 49.

2. [*Translator's note*: Japanese also has "kafukashiki."]

3. John Ayto, *Twentieth Century Words* (Oxford: Oxford University Press, 1999), 284. There are affinities between the "Orwellian" and the "Kafkaesque" in the sense that both are about phenomena of power.

4. Ayto, *Twentieth Century Words*, 283–84; *Penguin Encyclopedia*, ed. David Crystal (London: Penguin, 2006), 721. [*Translator's note*: See also *The Oxford Dictionary of Current English*, ed. Della Thompson (Oxford: Oxford University Press, 1996): "impenetrably oppressive or nightmarish," 483.] In his preface to the Pléiade edition of Kafka, Claude David proposes a beautiful definition of the French adjective "kafkaïen": "It entered language in order to describe these bureaucracies which organize themselves so well that they spin aimlessly in the void, in a rationality that spills over into the absurd." He adds the following commentary: "Isn't this stupid and cruel bureaucracy the very image of today's modern State? " See Claude David, "La Fortune de Kafka," in Franz Kafka, *Oeuvres complètes* (Paris: Gallimard, "La Pléiade," 1976), xi.

5. For instance I recently came across the case of Ora and Zelik Adler, French Jews naturalized after World War II who came respectively from Berlin and Warsaw, and who encountered insurmountable difficulties whey trying to renew their identity cards in France after the year 2000. The administration demanded not only their own birth certificates but also those of their parents. As Ora Adler commented: "It's Kafkaesque (*c'est kafkaïen*)." *Politis* 776 (September 17, 2003), 21.

6. See the commentary of Herbert Mills on *The Castle*: "Written from the point of view of the 'outsider' and the 'victim' of an organization, *The Castle* is in essence a superb psychological study of the individual facing a relentless, seemingly capricious, and presumably dangerous bureaucracy. The victim's experience takes on, under the magic of Kafka's art, a dreamlike, or, more properly, a nightmare quality. It is this quality . . . which captures in all of its starkness and terror what the 'uninitiated' individual may experience when obliged to deal with an organization. . . . The final stage of facing

an incomprehensible terror is reached when an 'Insider' explains to the victim that what he takes to be 'ludicrous bungling' is, on the contrary, the very embodiment of rationality. Unusual and extreme as this experience of Kafka's victim is, the reader is left with an unshakable conviction that the author has in no sense lost touch with the reality of an outsider's experience with bureaucracy but has, indeed, portrayed with consummate art a very real and very serious problem of modern life." Herbert Mills, *The Novelist on Organization and Administration: An Inquiry into the Relationship between Two Worlds* (Syracuse: Syracuse University Press, 1968), 114–15.

7. Michel Carrouges, "Dans le rire et les larmes de la vie," *Cahiers de la Compagnie Madeleine Renaud/Jean-Louis Barrault* 20 (October 1957), 19.

8. Milan Kundera, "Somewhere Behind," in Ruth Gross, ed., *Critical Essays on Franz Kafka* (Boston: G.K. Hall, 1990), 22–23.

9. Ibid., 25–26. Kundera is right in emphasizing that the kafkaesk universe is not a totalitarian one, since in his novels there is no party, nor ideology, nor secret police, nor any other element of totalitarian politics.

10. Ibid., 25.

11. Bernd Janowsky, "Bürokratie," in Erwin Grochia, ed., *Handwörterbuch der Organisation* (Stuttgart: C. E. Poeschel, 1969), 324.

INDEX